Michael Ondaatje's Fiction

Michael Ondaatje's Fiction

Poetics of Exile

Avinash Jodha

RAWAT PUBLICATIONS
Jaipur • New Delhi • Bangalore • Hyderabad • Guwahati

ISBN 978-81-316-0452-6

Published by
Prem Rawat for **Rawat Publications**
Satyam Apts, Sector 3, Jawahar Nagar, Jaipur 302 004 (India)
Phone: 0141 265 1748 / 7006 Fax: 0141 265 1748
E-mail: info@rawatbooks.com
Website: www.rawatbooks.com

New Delhi Office
4858/24, Ansari Road, Daryaganj, New Delhi 110 002
Phone: 011 2326 3290

Also at *Bangalore, Hyderabad* and *Guwahati*

Typeset by Rawat Computers, Jaipur
Printed at Chaman Enterprises, New Delhi

For

Jasbir Jain

my mentor

Contents

Preface

Dislocation is a theme of our times. The narratives of dislocation, the literature of the diasporas, and the poetics of exile has received substantial attention during the last few decades. Movement across and through geographical spaces and cultures exposes the otherwise unquestioned 'givens' that come with rootedness or location in specific nations, societies and cultures. The expatriate writers through their physical and multiple dislocations/relocations experience the cross-cultural influences, and are transformed by them as they transform the cultures and spaces they step in and step through. Appropriation, reappropriation and assimilation of diverse and discordant relationships have an important function in the expatriate experience, they work almost as imperatives and involve a certain amount of deliberation as the expatriate negotiates the contradictory claims and multiple pulls in his sense of being and belonging.

Michael Ondaatje is one of the few widely acclaimed expatriate writers. A Canadian poet and novelist, Ondaatje bears the influence of complex inheritances: his Sri Lankan Burgher background, education in Britain and the Canadian experience. Ondaatje has chosen a diverse range of subjects, and has located his works in Canada, Sri Lanka and in 'third' or neutral spaces. There have been multiple critical responses to his works. Critics have taken note of his thematic, narrative and structural strategies situating him within and outside different critical/theoretical frameworks. Ondaatje's criticism takes several directions and offers different vantage points but the perspectives fail to coalesce. Ondaatje's poetics demanded a deeper exploration, more crucially, from the perspective of the poetics of exile. This book concentrates on Ondaatje's multiple negotiations of identity, the manifestations of his cross-cultural inheritance and experience. While the central emphasis has been on his works of fiction, his poetry too has been brought into consideration. The focus is on identifying the literary strategies and devices that come to govern the immigrant writer's approach, the methodology he/she adopts to articulate the affinity and alienation from both the culture of origin and of adoption, the in-between states and his/her shaping of the new geographical and historical bearings.

The book is divided into six chapters. The first chapter is in the nature of an introduction. The second chapter takes up Ondaatje's involvement with myth and myth making. Ondaatje's negotiation of his belonging in the contexts of Canada and Sri Lanka has been considered in the third chapter. The fourth chapter explores Ondaatje's engagement with time and space and the narrative strategies he formulates to bring out his characteristic vision. The fifth chapter, grapples with the question of politics in the context of the expatriate experience, the conflict of contradictory allegiances and the corresponding responsibilities towards the country of adoption. The sixth chapter assesses the evolvement of Ondaatje's poetics in the context of contemporary expatriate writing.

Acknowledgements

The book has taken considerable research and time. I express my deepest gratitude to Professor Jasbir Jain who has been consistently supportive and encouraging. Her enthusiasm, intellectual depth and love have been a great source of inspiration for me. To know her as a person and to receive her guidance has been a great experience. I would like to thank Shastri Indo-Canadian Library, American Library, The British Council Library and JNU Library at New Delhi and Canadian Studies Centre, M.S. University, Vadodara for their support to my research. I wish to acknowledge my gratefulness to Cyril Dabydeen, M.J. Vassanji and Jean Arasanayagam, discussions with whom helped in important ways. I also thank my wife and my daughters for the love, respect and patience they have shown for my studies. My parents and younger brothers also deserve to be mentioned here as they kept up my spirits during this period.

1

Locating Dislocations

> A fugitive and wanderer shalt thou now henceforth live in this land, so long as thou shalt endure the light. Good people shall curse thee; thou shalt not ever come to the assembly of thy lord, exchange words there.
>
> Saxon *Genesis*

> Thou shalt be a diaspora in all the kingdoms of the earth.
>
> *Deuteronomy*

The exiles, the wanderers, and the immigrants, through ages, have traversed the fringes of the world. They have been the advertent/inadvertent carriers of their cultures across geographical divides, revealing civilisations in their affinities and contradictions. From the Jewish Diaspora of the Book to the contemporary political refugees and economic émigrés from the former colonies, the diasporas have come to signify "any group living in displacement".[1] However, the history of the exile, of dislocations and of the dislocated can be traced even further back than the Jewish expulsion. It is hardly a linear tradition or a homogenous body of the exiles' experience but it definitely is a tradition with a history as old as the formation of human societies on the earth.

Human societies have never been without their pariahs, prodigals, the willing and forced exiles. Etymologically 'exile' comes from the root "salire," to leap, thus: 'ex-silare' – to leap out. Being an exile is 'to leap out.' Generally understood, this leaping out signifies a *forced* physical move out of one's immediate geo-political and socio-cultural space but it can be subjective too; one example can be the persistent awareness of being locked in self-prisons as in T.S. Eliot's *Wasteland*. However, the term has a strong political connotation in the contemporary context whereby it signifies an establishmentarian or societal expulsion of an individual or group; or a departure forced by hostile or uncongenial circumstances. The terms exile, immigrant and expatriate have been used in contemporary discourses both interchangeably and to signify exclusive states of being.

Abdul R. JanMohamed identifies four different modes of border-crossings, "those used by the exile, the immigrant, the colonialist, and the scholar, the last typified by the anthropologist studying other cultures (one might add the tourist and the traveller as subcategories of the scholar/anthropologist)." He goes on to argue that "the notion of exile always emphasizes the absence of "home," of the cultural matrix that formed the individual subject"; therefore, "the nostalgia associated with the exile (a nostalgia that is structural rather than idiosyncratic) often makes the individual indifferent to the values and characteristics of the host culture … . The immigrant, on the other hand, is not troubled by the structural nostalgia because his or her status implies a purposive directedness towards the host culture, which has been deliberately chosen as the new home" (JanMohamed, 101).

The above categorisation is extremely intangible in nature and gets complicated if the other categories like refugee, expatriate and economic émigrés are taken into consideration. Bharati Mukherjee draws a line between immigrants and expatriates, "In my fiction, and in my Canadian experience, 'immigrants' were lost souls, put upon pathetic. Expatriates, on the other hand, knew too well who and what they were, and what foul fate had befallen them" (qtd. by Neil Bissoondath, 108). The contradictory positions of

JanMohamed and Bharati Mukherjee bring out the elusive nature of such categorisations. Very often these categories are based on the states of mind and the corresponding subjective postures and are seen through the binary of negative and positive attitudes towards the host culture but attitudes can certainly change and evolve.

The categories invariably overlap and admit of simultaneity. What brings the exile, immigrant, refugee and expatriate together is the experience of dislocation and this experience in its myriad forms has been manifested in the writings of the diasporas. The narratives of dislocation have been approached from multiple theoretical and critical perspectives. They have been studied from the larger perspectives of the theories of the formation of nation-states by the likes of E.P. Thompson, Ernest Gellner, Anthony Smith, E.J. Hobsbawm, Partha Chatterjee and Benedict Anderson. They have also been explored from the perspective of culture studies and from various racial, communal positions and discourses of marginality and resistance. Some of the major theorists in the field are Stuart Hall, Paul Gilory, Homi Bhabha, Rey Chow, Gayatri Spivak, Edward Said, William Saffran, Arjun Appadurai and R. Radhakrishnan (Vijay Mishra, 25). These theorists have located the experience and narratives of dislocation from different subject positions and have attempted to forge tenable frameworks of dislocations, marginalisations and resistances.

Dislocation can be situated in a broader context. Dislocation is a precondition of existence. From a psychological perspective coming into being is a dislocation; the severing of the natal cord signifies an individual's separation from the body of the mother and his/her simultaneous relocation in the body of the society. This relocation is only gradually realised but the initial dislocation remains and produces the Oedipal desire that has complex manifestations in an individual's relationship with society. Furthermore, the identification of the individual with society as an organic entity, the transference from the body of the mother to the body of the society, establishes a semblance of an organic relationship that if severed or abandoned produces a sense of loss, a desire to recuperate and repossess. The spiritual/religious theory of Genesis sees human existence on the earth as a state of perennial exile, the severing from God as a result of the original sin. The expulsion from the Garden of Eden and thereby from the body of God, envisions human existence as an act of desire, and hope whereby an individual keeps devising ways to be one with God again. Therefore, at one level dislocation, sense of loss and the desire to recuperate becomes the matrix of all existence.

The above matrix ostensibly under-runs all human existence but it has a blatant manifestation in the context of the exile, the diasporas and the immigrants as the severing of ties in their case has an immediacy that necessitates recognition and negotiation. The poetics of exile has a pervasive presence of a sense of loss but the nature of the pain largely depends on the individual's position in his/her society and the position of the society itself in the larger context of the nation states and the dominant racial, religious, cultural, economic and political global divides. The exile carries his/her culture in his physical being (the colour of the skin, physical stature – the racial denominators), and his subjective self to the host culture that perceives in him/her a contradiction to its foundational beliefs and sees a potential threat (Vijay Mishra, 25–30). The diasporas, as they look for a place in the host culture, have to face its fears that are manifested in multiple discriminations racial, social, economic and political. The discrimination can be direct or disguised in the several establishmentarian practices and the discourses of 'multiculturalism', but the effort largely is to keep the diasporas at bay while making a productive use of the individual skills of the diaspora communities.

The experience of relocation entails a continual crisis in the diasporic sensibility; the living reality of discrimination and the secondary status in the host countries consistently compel a simultaneous backward and forward glance. The crisis is multifariously objective and subjective that may lead to a deliberate drift into the past, or to a conscious forgetting of the past, a superimposition of the host culture; or to the possibility of working a way through a critical acceptance of the past and the present, refusing nothing and working out a sustainable sense of identity and being.

A sense of loss, discrimination, desire to belong, the struggle for recognition, empowerment and acceptance, in a broad way, can be seen as the common denominators of the poetics of exile. Vijay Mishra identifies the crucial significance of 'mourning', 'specter', 'identity' and 'trauma' in the experience of the diasporas (Vijay Mishra, 29); but beneath these common influences the poetics of exile admits an inherent heterogeneity, the subtle nuances of individual experience and the diverse manifestations and negotiations of the apparently common influences. The poetics of exile cannot be justly apprehended through extreme discursive positions of a universalistic discourse or through discourses of racial, communal and cultural exclusivism.

Michael Ondaatje's poetics in this context is an interesting point of departure towards a comprehensive understanding of the poetics of exile in its simultaneous homogenous and heterogeneous manifestations. Ondaatje inherits multiple racial, ethnic and socio-cultural hybridities. He belongs to the Sri Lankan Burgher community that has mixed Portuguese, Dutch, English, Sinhalese and Tamil lineages. In a way, the Burghers epitomise the colonial history of Sri Lanka in their multilateral ethnicities.

The Burghers owe their origin to the colonial strategy of the Portuguese and later the Dutch to make up for the shortage of (Portuguese and Dutch) women and to gradually evolve a community that may prove an effective tool in the maintenance of their stronghold in Ceylon. Later on the Burghers developed into two separate branches, the Dutch Burghers and the Portuguese Burghers. The Dutch Burghers were those who presumably had European ancestry in the male line and were 'white, Dutch reformed and Dutch speaking.' The Portuguese Burghers had a slightly uncertain European ancestry, had 'dark skins, were Catholics and spoke Creole Portuguese.' However, even these differences did not last long as there were intermarriages between these two branches of the Burghers and also there were some other European nationalities that kept pouring in and the settlers, though there were not many, got absorbed in the Burghers. With the British conquest of Ceylon in 1796, the Burghers were quick to adapt themselves to the ways of the new colonial power. Gradually they abandoned the use of Dutch language in favour of English and by the end of the nineteenth century there were not many Burghers who could claim the knowledge of Dutch language.

The end of the British regime in 1948 brought a complete reversal in the fortune of the Burghers as they lost most of their privileges and influence with the conversion of colonial Ceylon into independent Sri Lanka. The number of Burghers decreased drastically after independence as a large number of them migrated to countries like Australia and Canada. The immigration of the Burghers continued steadily and with the declaration of Sinhala, the official language of Sri Lanka in 1961 the Burgher population practically dwindled. There are still some Burghers in Sri Lanka and the Dutch Burgher Union of Ceylon still exists and so do the Dutch reformed Church under a new name the Presbytery of Ceylon. What remains are the relics of an affluent and glorious past and a rich multicultural heritage, a culture that evolved in the margins of history, at the cross-roads between the colonial powers from Europe and the natives of Ceylon.[2]

The Burghers were affluent, had positions of prominence in business and administration in the pre-independence era of Sri Lanka. Ondaatje's family too had a long line of ancestors who excelled in disciplines as various as medicine, law, botany and religion. Ondaatje writes about the arrival of his first ancestor on the island in his family memoir:

> my own ancestor arriving in 1600, a doctor who cured the residing governor's daughter with a strange herb and was rewarded with land, a foreign wife, and a new name which was a Dutch spelling of his own. Ondaatje. A parody of the ruling language. And when his Dutch wife died, marrying a Sinhelese woman, having nine children, and remaining. Here. At the center of the rumour. At this point on the map. (*Family*, 64)

With the passage of time Ondaatje's ancestry got further complicated as the Ondaatjes married into different communities. The Ondaatjes made some substantial contributions to the island in their different capacities while not being completely oblivious of their personal interests as they worked on the island. Ondaatje's grandfather Philip "Bampa" Ondaatje made a vast fortune by mediating between the British and the natives. He built the family home 'Rock Hill' that stretched in acres 'on a prime spot of land right in the center of the town of Kegalle' (Jewinski, 11). Michael Ondaatje spent his childhood in this house.

The complex nature of Burgher community, its alienation and the gradual dissipation signifies a distinctive history and experience.

Ondaatje's personal history – his community, the childhood experience of colonial Ceylon, his separation from his father, the subsequent journeys to England and to Canada, the British colonial education, exposure to the Canadian culture and literary tradition, the upheavals of family life – has found multiple manifestations in his works. His journeys across the continents and cultures have influenced his creative sensibility and the complex patterns of his individual experiences subtly merge in his literary journey over the years.

Ondaatje's literary journey began with the publication of his first collection of poetry, *The Dainty Monsters* in 1967 by Coach House. It is an anthology of poems written between 1963 and 1966 including the poems which won him the Ralph Gustafson Award in 1965, the Epstein Award and the E.J. Pratt Gold Medal for poetry in 1966 and the President's Medal at Western in 1967. *The Dainty Monsters* establishes some of the recurrent themes of Ondaatje. His fascination with animals, the webs of family connections and myth-making find expression in the poems with flashes of wit and an inherent comic impulse. *The Dainty Monsters* was followed by the long narrative poem *the man with seven toes* published in 1969 by Coach House; it received dramatic readings in Vancouver and Stratford.

The publication of *The Collected Works of Billy the Kid: Left Handed Poems* in 1970 brought Ondaatje into limelight. This curious collage of poetry, prose, photographs, comic book strips, excerpts from interviews added a new dimension to the legend of the famous nineteenth century American outlaw *Billy the Kid.* The book won him the Governor-General's Award for Poetry and Prose in 1970 and the Chamler's Award in 1973. It received dramatic production in theatres across the continent, in Toronto, Halifax, Vancouver, New York, Los Angles and Montreal. Ondaatje's study, *Leonard Cohen*, for McClelland and Stewart's *Canadian Writers Series* and his film on bpNichol *Sons of Captain Poetry* followed in 1971. Cohen had been an early influence on Michael, his *Beautiful Losers* had impressed Ondaatje and bpNichol was a friend and his poetic technique was a great source of interest for Ondaatje. In the same year Ondaatje, in collaboration with Tony Urquhart, a painter, brought out an anthology of poems and drawings entitled *The Broken Ark: A Book of Beasts.*

Rat Jelly, a collection of poems, was published in the year 1973. Divided in three sections, 'Families', 'Live Bait', and 'White Dwarfs'; the collection includes Ondaatje's poem for his father 'Letters & Other Worlds'. *Coming Through Slaughter,* which comes closer to the formal conception of novel, was published in the year 1976. The book revolves around Buddy Bolden, a pioneer jazz cornetist from New Orleans. Bolden was a black, he went mad in 1907 while giving a performance and spent the last twenty four years of his life in an asylum. Into its making went five years of research on Ondaatje's part and the book won Books in Canada Award for First Novel in 1976. *Elimination Dance* appeared in 1978. Relatively shorter the poem is a composition of diverse sentences, each followed by the drawing of a whip. Brilliant flashes of wit and irony mark every sentence and Ondaatje projects pressing private and public 'absurdities' that demand elimination.

There's a Trick with a Knife I'm Learning to Do, which selects pieces from the earlier collections and adds poems written up to 1978, was published in 1979. It contains some of the finest poems written by Ondaatje. The poems express an attempt to come to terms with submerged history. In the Asian poems of the volume, Ondaatje explores his family past and attempts to establish a connection between the past and present families and friends. The collection won Ondaatje a second Governor General's Award in 1979. This was followed by a period of travel and search. Ondaatje undertook two journeys to Sri Lanka in 1978 and in 1980; it resulted in *Running in the Family* (1982), not exactly a family memoir but what Ondaatje calls 'a gesture' that sought to 'touch into words' the 'frozen opera' of his parents' generation (*Family,* 22). The book brings in histories, legends and myths even as Ondaatje searches traces of his father and family in the picturesque landscape of his childhood. The book again eludes easy categorisation. In the same year another collection of Ondaatje's poems *Tin Roof* was published.

Secular Love (1984) is an intense, puzzling, disturbing yet strikingly beautiful collection of poems. Here Ondaatje, as Sam Solecki points out, involves himself in "the ruthless and unembarrassed engagement with the self" *(Spider Blues,* 125). The poems in the collection depict a deep down sense of despair that came from the breakdown of the poet's marriage. The collection presents Ondaatje caught up in contradictory emotions; on one side was the new love that he had discovered and on the other the inevitable of breakdown of his first marriage and his struggle to come to terms with the sense of guilt and failure to maintain his balance, his sanity.

In the Skin of a Lion focuses on the making of the city, Toronto was published in 1987. Set in the twenties and thirties, the novel gives the un-official story of the immigrants whose labour built the city and it also brings Ondaatje's immigrant perspective to bear upon the city. It is the first work by Ondaatje that fits in the generic demands of a novel. The Babylonian epic Gilgamesh from which the novel derives its title finds striking manifestations in the novel as Ondaatje uses the myth of Gilgamesh and comes up with a contemporary myth of his own. Through this elementary myth Ondaatje not only tears and looks into the skin of the official history of the making of Toronto but also focuses on the conflicts which the succession of skins brings, especially in a country which offers a confluence of cultures.

The Cinnamon Peeler: Selected Poems was published in Great Britain in 1989, United States in 1991 and Canada in 1992. The Booker Prize winning *The English Patient* (1992) followed. Set in Italy about the end of Second World War, the novel sweeps through times and places, boundaries and countries and invigorates the readers with its variousness. There are accounts of desert expeditions stretching back to Herodotus, a passionate love affair, deceit, guilt, suicide, the persecutions of identity and the attempts to escape it and the meeting of the continents as the characters find themselves in unlikely company enforced on them by the retreating war. *The English Patient* has the resonance of the myth of the Egyptian traveller in the form of the central character Almásy who is a reservoir of the fragmented accounts of expeditions through deserts. His own past is shrouded in dark, he is more 'the English Patient' than Almásy the other characters' identity too is bound more to the roles they play. Hana is 'the Nurse', Caravaggio is 'the Man with Bandaged hands', and Kip is 'the Sapper'. All these characters have travelled through countries, histories, boundaries. Ondaatje brings them together and puts them into a neutral space and through this confluence of cultures and identities moves a further step in his essential spatialisation of histories, countries and identities. Furthermore, the character of Kip, the Sikh soldier from India bears upon the novel the double perspective of the author. He is both looked upon from and looks through the white man's perspective. Along with the Booker the novel brought Ondaatje another Governor General's Award and the Trillium Award.

Handwriting (1998) and *Anil's Ghost* (2000) take Ondaatje back to Sri Lanka. The poems in *Handwriting* trace Ondaatje's relationship with the island that expands beyond the family relations to take into account the complex, variegated patterns of its history. While Ondaatje delves into the past of the island he also attempts to come to terms with its gory present. Some of the poems like "Wells", the second part of which is dedicated to the "ayah", are autobiographical in nature and resonates the family memoir *Running in the Family*. But as Sam Solecki remarks, "Handwriting swerves away for the most part from what could be called autobiographical concerns to a lyrical and multi-layered mosaic of a place and its complex histories." ("Recasting the Hand: Ondaatje's New Poems", *Books in Canada*, Nov./Dec., 1998)

Ondaatje's novel, *Anil's Ghost* like *Handwriting* brings an altered perspective to bear upon the island. Ondaatje searches meaning, sustainability and faith as his characters in the novel struggle to handle the chaos and the violence of the ethnic clashes in Sri Lanka. Ondaatje's earlier evasiveness of political issues gives way to a strong expression of concern for the island and its people. The novel does not take sides as Ondaatje sees 'blood on everyone's hands' nor does it offer any easy solutions. Ironically both the causes and the solutions lie buried in the past of the island and in the complex layers of human history. The novel juxtaposes simultaneous unearthing of the past and the burials of the present that reflect each other in curious ways. Both *Handwriting* and *Anil's Ghost* indicate Ondaatje's evolvement as a writer. From the personal and the familial he moves into the historical and the human. Both the books seek newer belongings beyond the obvious claims of nostalgia and personal ties.

Divisadero (2007), the latest novel by Ondaatje, is an artistic achievement of its own kind. The novel brings together the subtle layers of history, belonging, memory, intertextualities, search for the self and the need for escape. At the heart of the novel are France and California where Anna escaping a wound in memory embarks upon the task of piecing together the life of an evasive French writer as she traces a similar wound in the voice of the writer on a tape. The novel resonates the characteristic Ondaatjean strategy of bringing together an ensemble of characters who align themselves into shifting patterns of relationships and belonging. The story of the self leads into the diverse paths of others' stories and across the borders of history, memory and art and keeps coming back to the few climactic moments, the explosions and implosions that open unexpected pathways into future.

Ondaatje's critical and editorial work includes *Leonard Cohen* (1970) in the McClelland and Stewart *Canadian Writers Series*; *The Broken Ark: A Book of Beasts* (1971); *Personal Fictions: Stories by Munro, Wiebe, Thomas and Blaise* (1977); and *The Long Poem Anthology* (1979). The broadsides by Ondaatje include *In a Bangalore Stream (Quarry posters* No.5 Kingston: *Quarry,* 1968) *Philoctetes, on the Island (Unicorn Folio,* 3rd ser., No. I 'A Canadian Folio'), *To a Sad Daughter: For Quinton* Toronto: Coach House (1980).

Ondaatje has shown a serious interest in films. During the early 1970s, he produced a thirty-five minute film portrait of poet bpNichol *Sons of Captain Poetry* (1970); a comic short called *Carry on Crime and Punishment,* 1972 (16 mm; 5 min.), and a seventy-one minute documentary entitled *The Clinton Special*. Ondaatje has also written screenplays for Robert Kroetsh's novel *Badland* and his own *Coming Through Slaughter.* There have been dramatic productions of his works *the man with seven toes* (1968), *The Collected Works of Billy the Kid* (1971) and *Coming Through Slaughter* (1980). He was the editor of *Quarry,* 15, No. I, (September, 1965), No.3 (March, 1967) and he has been the editor of *From Ink Lake*: *Canadian Stories* (1990) and also the contributing editor of the literary journal *Brick* (Lecker and David, 130–136).

Ondaatje has evoked multiple responses. The critical responses, generally spread over several literary/academic journals, have taken into consideration various aspects of Ondaatje's writing. Critics have attempted to examine Ondaatje's poetics through the different theoretical/critical frameworks of postcolonialism, modernism and postmodernism, structuralism, culture, myth and gender criticisms. Ondaatje has been approached as a writer with remarkable technical skills. His ability to produce the desired result, often unsettling, through an apparently uncanny presentation of heterogeneous material – photographs, newspaper clippings, maps, poems, comic-book strips, the fragmented, disjointed narrative – has been a major temptation for the critics. Davey Frank in his book *From There to Here: A Guide to English Canadian Literature since 1960* calls Ondaatje, "a deliberate craftsman, firmly controlling the pace of his lyric poems". Ondaatje attempts "radical experiments" in writing technique. The narrative voice switches without overt signal and in his own defense he, "manipulates and watches, not only surviving, but creating a superbly tense, multicoloured, explosive macabre work ..." (*Our Nature – Our Voices*, Vol. 2, 222–227).

An interesting parallel between the process of photography and Ondaatje's treatment of the character of *Billy the Kid* is drawn by T.D. MacLulich in his article "Ondaatje's Mechanical Boy: Portrait of the Artist as a Photographer". He suggests photography as the controlling metaphor for both perception and artistic process in *Billy the Kid*. According to him photography supplies an apt metaphor for Billy's detached way of responding to the external world. The result is that the book offers a disturbing commentary on the far-reaching effects of that mechanical way of perceiving the world that is epitomised by the photographic process (*Mosaic* 14, No. 2,107–119).

In her article "Mapping and Masking: the Migrant Experience in Michael Ondaatje's *In the Skin of the Lion*", Susan Spearey examines some of the narrative strategies used by Ondaatje in the novel. She points out that Ondaatje deliberately undermines the notion of the linear and totalising account of events by pointing insistently to their simultaneity and to the reductive nature of confining narrative to a storyline. Michael Greenstien also takes note of the narrative structure of the novel that 'interception' and 'interruption' characterise two ways of proceeding through Ondaatje's text, "narrative pushes the reader forward while lyrical imagery turns around on itself". Greenstien suggests that the latter move involves, "a typically post-modernist self-reflexivity, which constantly draws attention to the boundaries within which the writer, reader and character alike are operating" (*Canadian Literature,* No. 126, 116–30, Autumn, 1990).

Rufus Cook observes, "Whether it is true of every "novel of memory" that it depicts human experiences as inherently "fractured" and discontinuous, it certainly is the case with Michael Ondaatje's *The English Patient.* Like Joy Kogawa's *Obasan* or Salman Rushdie's *Midnight's Children,* the book is filled with references to "fragments" or "gaps" or "shards", to "fractions" or "remnants", to characters who have been "dissembled" or "reassembled", to tapestries that have been "slashed apart", murals that have "crumbled away" (*Journal of Commonwealth Literature,* No. 2, 109–125, 1996).

Sam Solecki remarks, "He's among the handful of contemporary poets whom you can sense in almost any line of their work. In Canada, only Atwood has as strong a signature – an impress breathing in and through a line – colouring the work and establishing, constituting Camus' "climate." The climate of a world created book by book, never the same season, yet from *The Dainty Monsters* to *Running in the Family* always the same world" (*Spider Blues*, 334).

Ondaatje's name has surfaced as a likely candidate for the Nobel Prize, John Porter in his article "A Canadian Nobel Prize Winner" refers to Ondaatje as "a creator of a new art form an inventor of a style, a man who has founded his own literary country and keeps putting flags there lest anyone be mistaken" (*Academy of Canadian Writers Newsletter*, Vol. 2. No. 2, 1981)2. Ondaatje's new art form, according to Porter, is a collage of photography, poetry, interview, prose-narration and description, fairytale and biography.

Most of the critics of Ondaatje have taken special note of his compelling imaginary. Douglas Barbour in his review of the poetry collection *Dainty Monsters* finds the images, "obsessively natural", with, "a clear imaginative understanding of violence which never overwhelms the poet" (*Canadian Literature*, No. 36, 86–88, Spring 1968). Hugh MacCallum observes of the same book that Ondaatje's images are "hard" and "self-contained". Ondaatje writes about animals and birds as if intent on creating a modern bestiary or seeking to reproduce in words an effect similar to that achieved by primitivist painters (*University of Toronto Quarterly*, 37. 375, July, 1968). Some of the dominant images and the prevailing atmosphere in *The Collected Works of Billy the Kid*: *Left Handed Poems* are analysed by Peter Stevens in his review of the book. Stevens points out that Billy is framed as in a series of photographs which are blurred and browned by the nostalgia of time; images of "light and shadow recur, figures stand in the frame of black doorways and groups are described as in a pose". A camera's mechanism "freezes its subjects, lifting them in time from reality towards myth. Billy senses beauty within machinery ..." (*Queen's Quarterly*, Vol. 78, 326–327, Summer 1971). Leslie Mundwiler observes, "Ondaatje's poetry does not derive from or represent a memory system, but the structure of its imagery does bear a striking resemblance to the products of this creative mnemonics. Where the poems give a sense of place, the place is often a frame or architectonic background for image or images which are active, vivid, sensual, sometimes repulsive, painful or violent" (Mundwiler, 52).

Stephen Scobie in his article, "The Reading Lesson: Michael Ondaatje and the Patients of Desire" focuses upon the inevitability and potency of images in Ondaatje's works. He points out that Ondaatje's sensibility as a writer is grounded in poetry and all his novels may be described as "poetic novels." Rather than a character or plot Ondaatje begins his novels with an image. This image has all kinds of symbolic or mythological resonances. "The image unfolds, story begins and unwinds compellingly before us; and as Ondaatje slowly, deviously circles the plot back towards its opening climactic image ... the narrative grips us with a kind of horrified awe." With this central image comes a series of related images and out of these "two matrices of plot and image", emerges a cast of characters, each of them also balancing, mirroring, and complementing the others so that their total seems greater than the sum of their parts. These characters, "together form another image: a constellation ..." (*ECW*, No. 53, 92–106, Summer 1994).

Another persistent Ondaatjean concern is the question of identity, the vital relationship between the writer and his created other. Winfried Siemerling observes that Ondaatje probes 'the precarious balance – the limit of stability in the relationship between subject and object – between the perceiving, writing subjectivity and its created other.' For Ondaatje, he comes to the conclusion, "the relationship between poetic self and created other moves in a space between a 'mirrorstage' of recognition and a moment of distancing in which a degree of 'outsidedness' is restored" (Siemerling, 107–158).

Ondaatje's migrant status, his position as a front-rank Canadian writer, his Sri Lankan Burgher background and his consistent concern with movement and transformation has also called upon the attention of critics. Susan Spearey in her review of the novel *In the Skin of a Lion*, points out that the tropes of migration and metamorphosis recur in Ondaatje's novels as he explores textual, ideological, geopolitical and spatial boundaries, and as he investigates the multifarious and shifting subject positions occupied by the migrant. She points out that Ondaatje's is a 'poetics deeply engaged with movement and transformation with a pronounced concern with spatial dimensions' (*Journal of Commonwealth Literature,* No. 1, 45–59, 1995).

Most of the critics have also taken note of Ondaatje's move from poetry to novel writing, his acute awareness of generic borders and the consistent challenging of these borders in his narratives. Linda Hutcheon in her article "*Running in the Family*: The Postmodernist Challenge" remarks, "Of all the Canadian poets who have turned to fiction in the last few decades (Cohen, Atwood, Kogawa, Musgrave, and so on) Ondaatje is the one who is most aware of generic borders, and how they can be transgressed. Other writers have played about with the borders between the novel and the short story (Alice Munro, Ray Smith) and even poetry and fictional prose (Derk Wynand, Leonard Cohen), but Ondaatje takes such play one step further: beyond the boundaries of what we conventionally accept as *literary* genre and into history and biography" (*Spider Blues*, 32). Ina Ferris remarks, "For Ondaatje the shift to narrative has neither been simple nor unilateral (lyric enters significantly into his narratives), and the narratives he creates are of a peculiarly hybrid kind … . Ondaatje presents so illuminating a case of the postmodern writer who characteristically searches for but distrusts narrative structures, who seeks to connect words and world but remains unsure of either term or of whether they are two terms at all" (*Canadian Writers and their Works*, 75–83).

The treatment of violence in Ondaatje's works has invariably drawn the attention of the critics and there have been mixed responses towards Ondaatje's presentation and handling of violence in his poems and fiction. Comparing Ondaatje with other Canadian writers, Tom Marshall remarks, "If LePan's and Cohen's myths have to do with an expedition or descent into darkness, horror, a mystical sensuality, fragmentation and madness, then Michael Ondaatje's work could be said to carry this movement to a further, darker extreme. For here, there is virtually no intimation of the possibility of return or reintegration, of transcendence or the possible achievement of community (or even more than momentary communication), at least for the author's doomed heroes. Ondaatje's is, thus far, a darker and apparently more nihilistic vision than those of Watson, Klein, LePan, Cohen, MacEwen, Atwood, or Helwig, in whose work more positive human possibilities still exist even in the midst of darkness" (*Harsh and Lovely Lands*, 144). Christian Bök observes, "Michael Ondaatje has repeatedly demonstrated a writerly interest in violent, male protagonists who exhibit aesthetic sensitivity … . Violence in Ondaatje's work represents an aesthetic virtue, but whereas Ondaatje's earlier texts appear to valorize violence enacted for purely idiosyncratic reasons, Ondaatje's later texts begin to reevaluate the ethics of such violence and suggest that it must ultimately serve a socially responsible end" (*Canadian Literature*, 132, 109–124, 1992).

Ondaatje's works have also been approached from the gender perspective. Dennis Denisoff notes, "*Billy the Kid* is brimming with descriptions and hints that open the text up to a reading from a gay male perspective … the plethora of allusions to homosexuality and homosocial desire in *Billy the Kid* is intended not as a background for a conventional narrative reading or an essentialist social model; rather, the form and themes of *Billy the Kid* foster a reading of the text as a mutating body as well as a pluralist representation of social intercourse" (*ECW*, No. 53, 51–70, Summer 1994). Emphasising the absence of Ondaatje's criticism from a feminist perspective Lorraine M. York in "Whirling Blindfolded in the House of Women: Gender Politics in the Poetry and Fiction of Michael Ondaatje" remarks, "The feature of Ondaatje's writing that has, more than the use of stereotypes, kept the feminist analysis at a distance is what I would like to call "the male chaotic" – a realm of seemingly random, centrifugal violent energy, associated with males and either opposed or ignored by females." She refers to the predilection of the male critics for the 'penis metaphor' in describing Ondaatje's artist figures, although in Ondaatje's works there is subtle evolvement of the gender perspective. She traces Ondaatje's admiration of "breaking in" in the earlier works eventually giving way to a discomfort, an ideological aftertaste, "In fact, in recent works by Ondaatje, the woman as penetrated audience or object often turns creative – and that is enough to set patriarchal bridges of all kinds crumbling" (*ECW*, No. 53, 71–79, Summer, 1994).

Daniel Coleman refers to Ondaatje's *Running in the Family* and Ihab Hasan's *Out of Egypt* as, "... caught in a vast and intricate series of systems, they are, in fact, complicit in patriarchal-imperialist power structures. Nevertheless, their enormous value emerges in the way they articulate the contradictions and slippages that occur in the gender system when the autobiographical subject undergoes the dislocation of racial, national, and cultural identifications which is the narrative of emigration" (*SCL/ELC,* Vol. 17.2, 74, 1993). Karen Overbye in "Re-Membering the Body: Constructing the Self as Hero in *In the Skin of a Lion*" observes, "Foregrounding the body is one of the ways Ondaatje explores alternatives in fictional discourse. Rather than having the bodies in the novel represent something other than themselves (which immediately effaces them as "lived bodies"), Ondaatje reclaims them as sites of meaning, as extensions of the self. To a considerable extent, Ondaatje explores the role that the body plays in the development of the self, in how men regard their bodies, and, in the case of Patrick, how he reconciles his body and his self, and no longer completely adheres to the social models of masculinity" (*SCL/ELC*, Vol. 17.2. 12, 1993).

Ondaatje has reflected a deep interest in historical, legendary characters and in histories both private and public. Critics have examined Ondaatje's historical inclinations. Ajay Heble in "Michael Ondaatje and the Problem of History" observes, "Ondaatje has repeatedly been engaged in an attempt to incorporate marginal figures out of the historical past into a non-historical genre" (*Clio*,

No. 19. 97–100, Winter, 1990). Steven Totosy Zepetnek in "*The English Patient*: Truth is Stranger Than Fiction" remarks, "*The English Patient* is a postmodern text that succeeds in representing life – underlining its fullness, complicatedness, inexplicability, fragmentation, and subtextual richness, which cannot be represented by either traditional uses or a linear (fictional) narrative of historical 'facts'" (*ECW*, No. 53. 141, Summer 1994). Linda Hutcheon remarks, "Ondaatje is one of the few North American writers who address the issues of our immigrant, working-class history, a history silenced by official versions of public events" ("Ex-Centric", 132–35). Carol L. Beran in "Ex-Centricity: Michael Ondaatje's *In the Skin of a Lion* and Hugh Maclennan's *Barometer Rising*" observes, "... Ondaatje's choosing of historical events of local significance challenges the notion of history as a record of events of world significance and asserts the importance of marginalized events and relatively unknown people involved in them" (*SCL/ELC*, Vol. 16.2. 71–83, 1992). Fotios Sarris in "*In the Skin of a Lion*: Michael Ondaatje's Tenebristic Narrative" points out, "*In the Skin of a Lion* insists on the centrality of the human element in history. Only the inclusion of this element can bring about a proper understanding of both the past and the present, an understanding that may bring with it a recognition of a need for change" (*ECW*, No. 53, 183, Summer 1994).

Critics have repeatedly explored the influence of modern and postmodern techniques in Ondaatje's works. Douglas Barbour speaking in the context of Ondaatje's *Dainty Monsters* observes, "Indeed, in the shift from purely lyrical separate poems in the first section to sequences of poems in the second, it enacts one of the methods by which poetry made the shift from conventional modernism to postmodernism" ("The Last Time I wrote Paris: Ondaatje's First Attempt at a Poetic Sequence in Troy Town", 107). Leslie Mundwiler points out that Michael Ondaatje's work has visible traces of modernism though he goes beyond it, Ondaatje's work "presents us with the effects of modernism, the strengths of style and insight which can come from natural detail, but the basis of this way of experiencing is disjointed, failed in its logic, partially replaced by something else. In this respect and others; Ondaatje's belongs to a larger failure of coherence, the throes of modernism" (Mundwiler, 131). Bill Fledderus in "The English Patient Reposed in his Bed Like a (Fisher?) King: Elements of Grail Romance in Ondaatje's *The English Patient*", points out, "Ondaatje's use of the Arthurian grail quest and the more ancient narrative structures on which it is based – and ultimately most of the novel's basic elements – set themselves between modernism and postmodernism, exhibiting elements of both (e.g., its secularity and non-linear structure are postmodern, while its use of anthropology to suggest universal truths and its direct, un-ironic ties to some of its mythological source materials are modern)" (*SCL/ELC*. Vol. 22.1. 48. 1997). Danielle Miller in "Postmodernism: Bourgeois Smoke Screen of Ethical Philosophy: A Comparison of Michael Ondaatje's *Coming Through Slaughter* and Hubert Aquin's *Neige Noire*" criticises the superficial nature of postmodernism in *Coming Through Slaughter*, "... in *Coming Through Slaughter*, postmodernism, the supposedly noble and populist theory, becomes a smoke screen that pays lip service to the margins, either to reinforce their isolation, or to appropriate elements of their culture" (*British Journal of Commonwealth Studies*, Vol. 8, No. 2, 217, 1993).

Coomi S. Vevaina in her "Erasing Edges: Michael Ondaatje's *Coming Through Slaughter* and *Running in the Family* as Postmodernist Fiction" observes, "The writing of poet-novelist Michael Ondaatje shows the influence of "the connoisseur of chaos," Wallace Stevens, and of contemporary cinema artists like Louis Malle, Alfred Hitchcock and Sergio Leone. Fascinated by the strange and exotic, he tends towards the surrealistic dislocation of actuality and expresses the tensions in art and life in the form of fantastic narratives which border on the Gothic. His postmodernist affiliations cause him to resist the temptation of espousing any particular ideology or overriding system" (*Postmodernism and Feminism: Canadian Contexts*, 42).

Some of the critics have also taken note of Ondaatje's South Asian connection. Though, most of them find Ondaatje in a weak spot in this context. Arun Mukherjee in her article "The Poetry of Michael Ondaatje and Cyril Dabydeen: Two Responses to Otherness" castigates Ondaatje for his obliviousness of 'otherness,' apolitical stance and the elitist exoticism in his travel memoir

Running in the Family. She says, "Ondaatje's success has been won largely through a sacrifice of his regionality, his past and most importantly, his experience of otherness in Canada" (*Journal of Canadian Literature*, Vol. 20, No. I, 49–67, Spring, 1985). Chelva Kanaganayakam, though not completely subscribing to Arun Mukherjee's criticism, points out Ondaatje's failure in an impassioned involvement with contemporary events in Sri Lanka, "In his failure, Ondaatje shares the shortcomings of the majority of Sri Lankan writing in English which, for the most part, has stayed clear of the upheavals that have transformed a kindly, generous nation into a cruel and mindless battlefield" (*Canadian Literature*, Vol. 132, 33–34, 1992).

Ondaatje's romance with films, however, has not brought him a very favourable criticism. Expressing her views on Ondaatje's failure as a filmmaker Bart Testa in "He Did Not Work Here for Long: Michael Ondaatje in the Cinema" observes, "Michael Ondaatje was never a strong filmmaker, nor do his films constitute a substantial portion or significant extension of his accomplishment as an artist … . To be blunt about it, Ondaatje has expressed a vulgar taste in films … . Ondaatje's taste in popular cinema contrasts sharply with his literary preferences(for example, Wallace Stevens and Salman Rushdie) and with his preferences in the areas of painting (Greg Curnoe and Jack Chambers) and jazz (manifested in *Coming Through Slaughter* and elsewhere in his writings). His vulgar taste in films is not, I would surmise, a case of literary condescension but of genuine affection rooted in cinematic naivety" (*ECW*, No. 53, 154, Summer 1994). Though Leslie Mundwiler appreciates Ondaatje's effort, "*The Clinton Special* is a strong work, offering many levels of reflection on experience, art, and community. It deserves to be one of our most familiar films" (Mundwiler, 121).

The critical evaluation of Ondaatje takes different directions, the focus keeps shifting, there are several beginnings but the huge gaps in the present criticism become evident as one moves from one critic to another. Ondaatje has been simultaneously owned and disowned by the Canadian and Sri Lankan critics as 'one of their own'. Though the Canadian critical establishment has been largely approbatory in its response to Ondaatje; the long list of awards is ample evidence in itself, still there are some occasional dissenting voices but they remain significantly unheard in the overwhelming tone of praise. This is not to suggest that the praise is undeserved but both the critical gregariousness and skepticism require closer analysis.

Ondaatje has often been dealt with in parts and through pre-fixed frames of critical theories. The celebratory analysis of his technique, the strenuous efforts to situate him within modernist or postmodernist traditions, becomes a mechanical tug of war between theories and misses out on the subtle nuances of Ondaatje's poetics. The apparently fragmentary nature of Ondaatje's narratives has had a metaphoric influence on his criticism and even some of the best critical explorations of the individual aspects of his poetics fail to provide an insight into his poetics as a whole.

The limitations of Ondaatje's criticism, the absences and the missing links, foreground the complex nature of the poetics of exile that cannot be comprehensively apprehended through standardised theoretical/critical perspectives. There are obvious fissures even in the expatriate theories, postcolonial or otherwise, that though supposedly resistant to hierarchies and binary divisions, resort to the First, Second and Third World divides; stereotyping them as cultural equivalents offering homogenous patterns of the exile's experience. The different theoretical frameworks are helpful in opening some of the vital issues in expatriate writing but their compromise to their corresponding frames leaves splits wide open that demand a deeper negotiation.

Ondaatje's poetics demands, from a critical standpoint, a step further than the isolatory critical strategies and explorations, a conglomeration of various perspectives that may help in an understanding of the underlying unity of his imaginative and creative sensibility. This book concentrates on Ondaatje's poetics vis-à-vis the poetics of exile. It traces Ondaatje's evolvement as a poet and a novelist from *The Dainty Monsters* to *Divisadero*. The attempt has been to understand and analyse Ondaatje's aesthetics as an expatriate writer. The focus is, as already detailed above, on identifying the fundamental aspects of the expatriate experience, his/her engagement with personal, communal, cultural and national histories, the negotiation of multifarious subject positions, the challenge of multiple belongings and corresponding allegiances; the struggle for acceptance and empowerment, and the evolvement of a sustainable sense of identity.

Notes

1. The definition appears in *Oxford English Dictionary.* Here it has been quoted from Vijay Mishra's, "Diasporas and the Art of Impossible Mourning". *In Diaspora: Theories, Histories, Texts*. Ed. Makarand Paranjape, Indialog, 2001.
2. Some of the references to the history of the Burghers in Ceylon are from Ramerini, Marco. "History of the Dutch in Ceylon (Sri Lanka): The Burgher of Ceylon", www.lankalibrary.com

Works Cited

Barbour, Douglas. 'The Last Time I wrote "Paris": Ondaatje's First Attempt at a Poetic Sequence in "Troy Town"' *ECW* 53 (Summer, 1994): 107.

——. "Controlling the Jungle." *Canadian Literature* 36 (Spring, 1968): 83–88.

Beran, Carol L. "Ex-Centricity: Michael Ondaatje's *In the Skin of a Lion* and Hugh Maclennan's *Barometer Rising*" *SCL/ELC*, Vol. 16.2 (1992): 71–83.

Bissoondath, Neil. "The Uses of Ethnicity", *Selling Illusions: The Culture of Multiculturalism in Canada*. Toronto: Penguin 1994.

Bök, Christian. "The Politicization of Violence in the Works of Michael Ondaatje." *Canadian Literature*. 132 (1992): 109–24.

Coleman, Daniel. "Masculinity's Severed Self: Gender and Orientalism in *Out of Egypt* and *Running in the Family*". *SCL/ELC* Vol. 17.2 (1993): 63–79.

Cook, Rufus. "Imploding Time and Geography": *Narrative Compressions in Michael Ondaatje's* The English Patient". *Journal of Commonwealth Literature*. No.2. (1996):109–125.

Davey, Frank. "Michael Ondaatje (1943)." In his *From there to Here: A Guide to English Canadian Literature since 1960.* Vol. II of *Our Nature – Our Voices*. Erin, ant.: Porcepic (1974): 222–27.

Denisoff, Dennis. "Homosocial Desire and the Artificial man in Michael Ondaatje's *The Collected Works of Billy the Kid*". *Michael Ondaatje Issue, ECW* 53 (Summer, 1994): 51–70.

Ferris, Ina. "Michael Ondaatje and the Turn to Narrative". *Canadian Writers and Their Works*. Ed. Robert Lecker, Jack David, Ellen Quigley. ECW Press, 1992.

Fledderus, Bill "The English Patient Reposed in his Bed Like a (Fisher?) King: Elements of Grail Romance in Ondaatje's *The English Patient*". *SCL/ELC*. Vol.22.1 (1997): 48.

Greeenstein, Michael. "Ondaatje's Metamorphoses: *In the Skin of a Lion*". *Canadian Literature*. No. 126 (Autumn, 1990): 116–130.

Heble, Ajay. "Michael Ondaatje and the Problem of History". *Clio*. No. 19 (Winter, 1990): 97–100.

Hutcheon, Linda. "*Running in the Family*: The Postmodernist Challenge". *Spider Blues*. Ed. Sam Solecki. Montreal: Vehicule Press, 1985. 301–14.

——. "Ex-Centric". *Canadian Literature*. 1147 (1988): 132–35.

JanMohamed, Abdul R. "Worldliness-without-World, Homelessness-as-Home: Towards a Definition of the Specular Border Intellectual", *Edward Said: A Critical Reader*. Oxford: Blackwell. 1992.

Kanaganakayam, Chelva. "A Trick With Glass: Michael Ondaatje's South Asian Connection". *Canadian Literature*. Vol. 132 (1992): 33–34.

Lee, Dennis. *Savage Fields: An Essay* in *Literature and Cosmology*. Toronto: House *of* Anansi, (1977). pp. 4. 15–60, 115–22.

MacLulich, T.D. "Ondaatje's Mechanical Boy: Portrait of the Artist as Photographer". *Mosaic: A Journal for the Comparative Study of Literature and Ideas* 14, No.2 (Spring, 1981): 107–19.

MacCallum, Hugh. "Letters in Canada: 1967 Poetry". *University of Toronto Quarterly*. Vol. 37 (July, 1968): 375.

Marshall, Tom. *Harsh and Lovely land: The Major Canadian Poets and the Making of a Canadian Tradition*. Vancouver: University of British Columbia Press, (1979). pp. xiv, 112, 123–26, 144–47, 149, 15,354, 163–64,167–70,172.

Miller, Danielle "Postmodernism: Bourgeois Smoke Screen of Ethical Philosophy. A Comparison Michael Ondaatje's *Coming Through Slaughter* and Hubert Aquin's *Neige Noire*". *British Journal of Commonwealth Studies*. Vol. 8 No. 2 (1993): 217.

Mishra, Vijay. "Diasporas and the Art of Impossible Mourning", *In Diaspora: Theories, Histories, Texts*. Ed. Makarand Paranjape. Indialog, 2001.

Mukherjee, Arun. "The Poetry of Michael Ondaatje and Cyril Dabydeen: Two Responses to Otherness". *Journal of Canadian Literature*. Vol.20, No. I. (Spring, 1985): 49–67.

Mundwiler, Leslie. *Michael Ondaatje: Word, Image, Imagination*. Vancouver: Talonbooks, 1984.

Nodelman, Perry. "The Collected Photographs of Billy the Kid". *Canadian Literature*. No. 87 (Winter, 1980): 68–79.

Ondaatje, Michael. *The Dainty Monster*. Toronto: Coach House, 1967.

——. *The man with seven toes*. Toronto: Coach House, 1969.

——. *The Collected Works of Billy the Kid. Left Handed Poems*. Toronto: House of Anansi, 1970.

——. *Leonard Cohen. Canadian Writers Series,* No. 5. Toronto: McClleland and Stewart, 1970.

——. Ed. *The Broken Ark:* A Book of Beasts. Ottawa: Oberon, 1971.

——. *Rat Jelly*. Toronto: Coach House, 1973.

——. *Coming Through Slaughter*. Toronto: House of Anansi, 1976.

——. Ed. *Personal Fictions: Stories by Munro, Wiebe, Thomas and Blais*. Toronto: Oxford Univ. Press, 1977.

——. Ed. *The Long Poem Anthology*. Toronto: Coach House, 1979.

——. *There's a Trick With a Knife I'm Learning to Do. Poems* 1963–1978. Toronto: McClelland and Stewart, 1979.

——. *Running in the Family*. Toronto: McClelland and Stewart, 1982.

——. *Secular Love*. Toronto: Coach House, 1984.

——. *In the Skin of a Lion*. Toronto: McClleland and Stewart, 1987.

——. *The Cinnamon Peeler:* Selected Poems, 1989. Toronto: McClelland, 1992.

——. Ed. *From Ink Lake: Canadian Stories*. Toronto: Lester & Orphen Dennys, 1990.

——. *The English Patient*. Toronto: McClelland and Stewart, 1992.

——. *Handwriting*. Toronto: McClelland and Stewart, 1998.

——. *Anil's Ghost* (2000). Picador India, 2000.

——. *Divisadero*. London: Bloomsbury, 2008.

Overbye, Karen. "Re-Membering the Body: Constructing the Self as Hero in *In the Skin of a Lion*", *SCL/ELC*. Volume 17.2 (1993):12.

Porter, John. *Academy of Canadian Writers Newsletter*. No. 2, February 1981.

Sarris, Fotios. "*In the Skin of a Lion*: Michael Ondaatje's Tenebristic Narrative". *ECW*. No.53 (Summer, 1994): 183.

Scobie, Stephen. "Two Authors in Search of a Character". *Canadian Literature*, No. 54 (Autumn, 1972): 37–55.

——. "The Reading Lesson: Michael Ondaatje and the Patients of Desire". *ECW*. No. 53 (Summer, 1994): 92–106.

Solecki, Sam. "Nets and Chaos: The Poetry of Michael Ondaatje". *Studies in Canadian Literature*. Vol. 2 (Winter, 1977): 36–48.

——. "Michael Ondaatje: A Paper Promiscuous and Out of Form with Several Enlargements and Untutored Narrative". *Descant*. 14.4 (1983): 77–78.

Spearey, Susan. "Mapping and Masking: The Migrant Experience in Michael Ondaatje's *In the Skin of the Lion*". *Journal of Commonwealth Literature*. No.1. (1995):45–59.

Stevens, Peter. "Rev. of *Collected Works of Billy the Kid*". *Queens's Quarterly*. Vol. 78 (Summer, 1971): 326–27.

Sugunasiri, Suwanda H.J. "Sri-Lankan Canadian Poets: The Bourgeoisie that Fled the Revolution". *Canadian Literature*. Vol.132 (1992): 60–79.

Vevaina, Coomi S. "Erasing Edges: Michael Ondaatje's *Coming Through Slaughter* and *Running in the Family* as Postmodernist Fiction". *Postmodernism and Feminism: Canadian Contexts*. Ed. Shrin Kudchedkar. Pencraft International: 42)

Testa, Bart. "He Did Not Work Here for Long: Michael Ondaatje in the Cinema". *ECW*. No. 53. (Summer, 1994): 154.

York, Lorraine M. "Whirling Blindfolded in the House of Women: Gender Politics in the Poetry and Fiction of Michael Ondaatje". *ECW*. No.53 (Summer, 1994): 71–79.

Zepetnek, Stevens T. "*The English Patient*: "Truth is Stranger Than Fiction". *ECW*. No. 53 (Summer, 1994): 141.

2

'His Legend a Jungle Sleep'*

Myth and Myth Making

Michael Ondaatje has shown a profound interest in myth and myth making. His interest in myths and the poetic possibilities they offer can be traced back to the subject of his M.A. thesis, "Mythology in the Poetry of Edwin Muir: A Study of the Making and Using of Mythology in Edwin Muir's Poetry" (1967). He was particularly fascinated by the potency of myths. In the *Manna* interview, Ondaatje speaks out:

> I am interested in myth. Making it, remaking it, exploding (it). I don't like poems or works that cash in on a cliché of history or personality ... Myths are only of value to me when they are realistic as well as having other qualities of myth. Another thing that interests me about myth is how and when figures get caught in myths. (qtd. by Jewinski, 46)

In the M.A. thesis, Ondaatje closely examines Muir's linking of personal experience to larger myths of universal value. He underlines the immediate and private, the mythic, and the historic as the three possible means of connecting the personal to the universal. "For him" remarks Ed Jewinski, "these three levels formed a template with which to gauge the universal" (Jewinski, 46). The thesis reveals

---

* This is from Michael Ondaatje's *Billy the Kid* (*The Collected Works of Billy the Kid*, 67).

Ondaatje's interest in 'mythos, archetypes and universals' and his characteristic concern for situating/blending the individual experiences with the larger frameworks offered by myths. Ondaatje points out in his abstract: "I discuss the poems where Muir made myths: out of his own life, his insights into Eden and the Fall, and his visions and dream" (Jewinski, 47). Though at this juncture, Ondaatje's fascination with myth served him an academic purpose, it was to become a formative influence and an essential constituent of his aesthetics as a creative writer. In the works that followed Ondaatje was to develop a more coherent approach towards mythology and myth making and towards discovering a poetic voice.

The term 'myth' poses a problem, the problem of arriving at an agreeable definition avoiding both the generalisational or analytical extremes. The difficulty is compounded by the close association of myth with terms like legend, saga, and folktale. These categories often overlap and are used synonymously with myth. However, despite all contradictions, myth's fascination, significance and influence stand undeniable. There have been attempts to define myth from anthropological, psychological, religious, sociological and several other perspectives as it occupies a substantial position in each area of study. The comprehension of Ondaatje's handling of myths and his myth making demands an exploration some of the ways in which myths have been used over a period of time.

Some of the key theories and theorists in the interpretation of myths have been: the nineteenth century universal theory propounded by Max Müller, the twentieth century psychological theories by Freud and Jung, H.J. Rose's theory of the myths of primitive and sophisticated societies, the anthropological theories proposed by Sir J.G. Frazer, Bronislav Malinowski and the structural theories proposed by Claude Levi-Strauss and Northrop Frye. Each of these theories have explored the dynamism of myth from different perspectives and its powerful influence on the matrix of the individual, society, religion and human existence in its affinities and contradictions and the constant struggle between the material and the metaphoric.

The juxtaposition of different theories reveals that myth, like truth is absolutely relative containing within its complex structures multiple connotative intricacies that may partially be revealed in a given set of social complex and at a given point of time. There can be no single version of myth and that all versions are true because myth like society is a living organism in which all the constituent parts contribute to the existence of the whole. Myths are kaleidoscopic in nature, each turn reveals amazingly distinctive patterns that realign, readjust, obtain the foreground or retreat to the background with each movement of the device. Similarly historical facts, social customs, beliefs, rites, rituals, collective unconscious or individual suppressed selves, natural, religious phenomenon, are all but constituents of myth which realign and rearrange into new relationships to form the mythical wholes completely distinctive in each cultural, social context. Myths evolve, live and breathe, grow, get old and die and are reborn, rejuvenated and reincarnated. They also travel and go through metamorphosis. They tenaciously hold on to the human imagination as they offer vibrancy, vigour, variegated patterns and elemental structures of human emotions and situations.

Fundamentally myths have always worked at least in three ways:

(i) they have helped to crystallise the wisdom of a community through some belief, model or narrative;
(ii) they have become means of cultural continuity and have thus transformed themselves into carriers of meaning; and
(iii) their repetition acquires symbolic importance.

Further, myths are often a medium of the process of socialisation. They carry within them the capacity to shrink to a nodal point as well as the ability to expand. Interest in myths, though a perennial one, has resurfaced from time to time and more significantly in the context of cultural crisis. The publication of Frazer's *The Golden Bough* gave an extra spur to the mythopoic tendency and T.S. Eliot's *The Wasteland* is a testimony to this, a work critical of the post-First World War scenario. It is important to consider how myths of one culture go through multiple transformations as they transgress into other cultures.

The cross-cultural travels of myths provide them a syncretic texture as they are homogenised by other cultures. In the colonial and the postcolonial contexts myths have performed divergent functions. They have been used to perpetuate the superior/inferior divide between the coloniser and the colonised and they have also served to counter domination whereby the colonised cultures have used the western myths to address crisis in their own worlds. In the contemporary context, with rapid globalisation, and the increasing inter-cultural exposures and influences myths have acquired a complex hybridity. Myths now have an extensive range right from spiritual concerns to life-styles and mental attitudes.

Literature draws its structural principles from myth and transmutes them into complex manifestations. Writers, for ages, have resorted to the use of myth and the literary uses have either been rewritings or reinterpretations. Ondaatje in *The Collected Works of Billy the Kid: Left Handed Poems* (1970) turns not to a native myth, that is, belonging to his culture of origin, but to Billy the Kid, a cultural myth of the Northwest. Ondaatje's move demands multiple readings – from his subject position of a Canadian choosing to deal with an American cowboy myth in the 70s, his association with the myth from the standpoint of his childhood in colonial Ceylon and from the larger context of inter-cultural appropriation of the cowboy myth and its contemporary reflections in the swift globalising of the world and its cultures.

A fuller understanding of Ondaatje's involvement in the legend of Billy the Kid at a mythic level and the implications of his treatment requires in the first place, an understanding of the background of the 'Wild Wild West'. In both the historical West and the West in the popular imagination lie the seeds of Billy's creation. He mediates between these two worlds, the factual and the fantastic, the historic and the mythic. The symbolic worth of the West rises far above its geographically diverse domain. Initially, the quest for the West was the quest for India; the pioneers of white settlements, through the path of civilisation, trying to accomplish what Columbus sought and could not. With the likes of Daniel Boone it became a quest for unrestricted freedom, an escape from civilisation into wilderness (*Virgin Land*, 19).

The West with its large unclaimed, unoccupied territory, geographical hazards, and Indians became a place where only the mighty, the brave and the desperate may venture and the New World offered many such men. Large stocks of wild cattle brought the cowboys and their masters, the rich landowners to the forefront. It became a question of capturing and holding as many as you could and guiding them safely to the far away railheads through the long trail. With it began the cowboy era and the legends drawing within them the roughness of the locale, adventurousness of the pioneers, savagery of the Indians and a potpourri of tales and motives that travelled from the Old World to the New with the cowboys and the settlers.

The actual cowboy era lasted roughly for about three decades, from the end of the Civil War in 1865 to 1900. By the turn of the century the cowboys had already become extinct. The hostility and the roughness of the 'Wild, Wild West' were matched by an unmistakable streak of violence. Fostered by the slackened grip of law, the gun became the strongest mode of communication, almost an essential tool of survival. Outlaws, bandits and raiders were a common feature of the era. In the widely scattered habitations of the open country the people adapted themselves to the violent demands of life.[1]

The reasons behind this plethora of violence ranged from slavery to claims over unclaimed territories and from cattle to losing bets in the bars. *The Reader's Digest Book of American Folklore and Legend* relates:

> In the Kansas-Missouri border fighting that raged 20 years before, during and after the Civil War, slavery was the original issue, but as conflict broadened to involve every man, woman and child, the reasons, for it all became very complex. On both sides a lynch-mob mentality developed. The circumstances brought, men like Confederate William Quantrill's murderous "irregulars" to the forefront, and from the gunsmoke emerged bandit hero Jesse James, a Quantrill veteran. His legend was soon rivaled by those of the younger Sam Bass and Billy the Kid. All have a common resemblance to Robin Hood; all were betrayed by friends. (315)

However hard might have been the life of a cowboy and however short his era might have been, yet the fact remains that there was something in his loneliness, independence, the toughness of his task and his casual attitude towards life which has sustained his image in the popular imagination till today. The dime novels, which began to appear in 1860s, popularised the cowboy legend. Most significant of these dime novelists was Ned Buntline; the popularity of his novels initiated the movie westerns and the western fiction. Subsequently, the arrival of the authors like Owen Wister and Andy Adams not only made it a serious literary genre but also set the tone for the movie westerns which used the situations of these novels with some modifications and gained immense popularity.

Today, the word 'cowboy' summons up images of a rough, brave, trigger-happy, independent loner, in a rugged outfit, riding an equally rugged horse, with all the signs of a long drive, yet perfectly poised with an unfailing calm expression on his face, ready to burst into action with the pistols at his hips and a ready supply of bullets, operating in an era in which the law was as arbitrary as crime itself with no clear lines of distinction between lawmen and outlaws. This image of the cowboy and his environment of the 'Wild Wild West' have largely been established through the popular 'westerns,' the movies and novels. In fact they have played a central role in romanticising and mythologising the cowboy charisma.

The sustenance of the cowboy legend has something more to it than just movies or novels. From a psychological point of view it appeals to that part of our inner self that craves for a cowboy-like freedom far away from the hackneyed business of life, the adventure, the casualness and the rudimentary forms of crime and punishment. The cowboy legend becomes an objective correlative for a part of our inner suppressed selves hence its popularity and lasting value. In some ways it is this part of our nature that was objectivised in the Hippie movement of the 60's and the popular songs of the Rock stars in the 70's and 80's in which hitch-hiking on the highway became the metaphor for life.

Out of this whole range of potentially legendary characters, Michael Ondaatje chooses the figure of Billy the Kid. The question arises, why Billy? Why not one from the others or for that matter his Canadian counterparts Louis Riel or Paul Rose? The ultimate answer lies perhaps deep within the psyche of the writer himself but there are both biographical and textual evidences, which give some clues to Ondaatje's choice of Billy as his subject. As a child in Ceylon, Ondaatje sought a great relief in the newly imported American pop culture, from his strictly, British-colonial education and family environment. Ed Jewinski in his biography of Ondaatje *Express Yourself Beautifully* (1994) relates how Michael accompanied his uncle Noel to see Gene Autry and Roy Rogers films (22). He also showed a great passion for American comic books, especially those in the series entitled *Frontier News,* which glamorised the lore of the Wild West. In an interview to Pearl Sheffy Gegen of the *Globe and Mail,* Ondaatje admits, "By the age of 8, the germ of the Western was in me and I dragged myself to see every movie made about Billy (the kid) .... I grew up with this mythology of movies and comic books that came all the way from America to this tropical island" (Jewinski, 22).

Ondaatje held a great fascination for the movie westerns and the American comic books that glorified and romanticised the cowboy era. Yet it was the figure of Billy the Kid, as the above quote from his interview indicates, which captured Ondaatje's childhood imagination particularly. Whether it was the youth of William Bonney (Billy) or his Kid status, the grimness of his humour or the impossibility of his situation or the whole mythical aura that surrounds his figure that attracted Ondaatje's attention it is difficult to envisage. Yet one thing that stands out clearly is that amid all his fascination for the 'Wild Wild West' it was Billy the Kid who loomed large over Ondaatje's imagination and struck some hidden chords in him.

Ondaatje sustained his childhood interest in the West and in Billy. Some of his favourite films have been Sergio Leone's mythic *Once Upon a Time in the West* and Arthur Penn's *The Left Handed Gun*. Significantly enough the subtitle of Ondaatje's *Collected Works of Billy the Kid* is *Left Handed Poems.* Thus, to some extent, as Stephen Scobie remarks, Ondaatje's *The Collected Works of Billy the Kid,* is "a natural outgrowth from his love of Hollywood (and Italian) westerns" (*Poets and Critics*, 225). Yet, however, strong may have been these personal reasons for a writer of Ondaatje's maturity they could not be the only ones. A determination of the extent to which *The Collected Works of Billy the Kid* becomes an expression of Ondaatje's personal, artistic and aesthetic concerns, requires a close examination of his treatment of the Billy legend, a legend treated by many authors before him allowing the legend to grow and transform.

The first two decades that followed Billy's death, witnessed writers over-stressing their abilities in creating increasingly extravagant pictures of Billy's villainy. He became 'a devil incarnate, a paragon of evil.' But the change of the century brought a reversal in the fortunes of Billy. He was now drenched with profuse showers of sentimentalism and presented as a victim rather than as a victimiser. The writers concocted all sorts of justifications for the murders by Billy and gradually Billy emerged as a folk-hero of the Robin Hood variety (*Poets and Critics*, 227).

The popularity of the dime novelists like Ned Buntline and Owen Wister prompted many writers, with average literary skills, to try their hands at Billy. Some of the books produced upon the subject are: *The True Life of Billy the Kid* by Don Jenardo (1881); *The Authentic Life of Billy, the Kid* by Pat Garrett (ghost-written by Ash Upson) (1882); *Billy the Kid, The True Story of a Western 'Bad man'* by Emerson Hough (1901); *The Saga of Billy the Kid* by Walter Noble Burns (1926): *The Real Billy the Kid* by Miguel Otero (1936); *The Authentic Death of Hendry Jones* by Charles Neider and *The True Story of Billy the Kid* by William Lee Hamlin (1959). The titles of these books and the years of publication suggest a consistently maintained long tradition of presenting the Billy legend under a highly palpable disguise of historical authenticity. Kent Ladd Steckmesser simply classifies these pseudo 'true' and 'authentic' histories as the strenuous creations of 'The Satanic Billy' or 'The Saintly Billy' (*Poets and Critics*, 228).

In 1930 the first Hollywood film version of the legend appeared but they too strived for a similar air of authenticity. The signs of a positive development in the tackling of the legend surfaced with works like Samuel R. Delany's novel, *The Einstein Intersection*, in which Billy appears as 'Bonny William' or 'Kid Death,' and Michael McClure's play *The Beard*. These works along with movies like Arthur Penn's *The Left Handed Gun* (1960), starring Paul Newman attempted to explore Billy the Kid legend from a mythological perspective. Michael Ondaatje's approach towards the legend in his *The Collected Works of Billy the Kid; Left Handed Poems* is more akin to these later matures approaches.

As far as bringing about the 'true', 'authentic,' or 'historical' image of Billy is concerned, Ondaatje did not bother himself much. Whittaker quotes Ondaatje as saying that he was never "interested in the real Billy the Kid. In fact, I think he was probably a dull, boorish character" (Jewinski, 65). A comparison of this statement with the claims of the writers like Pat Garrett reveals the true 'artistic worth' of Ondaatje's work. For instance, Pat Garrett in his *Authentic Life* claims, "I have listened, at campfires, on the trail, in the prairies and at many different plazas, to his discontented relations of events of his early and more recent life" and therefore he finds himself in a position to "safely guarantee that the reader will find in my little book a true and concise relation of the principal interesting events therein, without exaggeration or accusation." Garrett at the same time is confident that his work would be able "to correct the thousand false statements which have appeared in the public newspapers and in yellow covered cheap novels" (*Poets and Critics*, 228–229).

Another interesting example of these 'authentic' approaches toward Billy may be seen in the highly dramatic terms in which Sir Walter Noble Burns describes Billy in his book *The Saga of Billy the Kid*:

> Fate set a stage. Out of nowhere into the drama stepped this unknown boy. Opposite him played Death. It was a drama of Death and the boy. Death dogged his trail relentlessly. It was forever clutching at him with skeleton hands. It lay in ambush for him. It edged him to the gallows stairs. By bullets, conflagration, stratagems, every lethal trick, it sought to compass his destruction. But the boy was not to be trapped. He escaped by apparent miracles: he was saved as if by necromancy. He laughed at Death. Death was a joke.
>
> (*Poets and Critics*, 227)

Ondaatje could not appreciate such approaches toward Billy. In fact, the whole nature of the works produced upon Billy gave Ondaatje an uneasy feeling. In an interview to Catherine Bush, he points out, "I was sick of all clichés the hip versions of him that reduced the danger of such character. I wasn't interested in appropriating him as a mythic figure, it was much more of a personal enquiry" (Jewinski, 66). Ondaatje's *Collected Works of Billy the Kid* does not attempt to reclaim or to justify Billy against the backdrop of ingenuously created facts and situations but on the contrary it extends its grasp beyond historicity and works upon the levels of mythology and myth making. Ondaatje reaches out to the poetic truth and the justifications, if any, lie within the framework of the book.

It is important to see how far Ondaatje subscribes to the details, historical and legendary, accumulated around Billy. The historical and legendary versions of Billy lay a great emphasis on Billy's exploits that is the tale begins with Billy murdering a man for insulting his mother at the age of twelve and later getting farther and farther away and leaving a long trail of heroic/villainous shootouts and escapades. Ondaatje in place of delving into the details of the Lincoln Country War when Billy the Kid was at his best, concentrates on a time when the war is already over and Garrett is on his trail. As for the earlier exploits Ondaatje makes Billy give a matter of fact list of the murders committed by each side:

> These are the Killed.
> (By me)
> Morton, Baker, early friends of mine.
> Toe Bernstein. 3 Indians.
> A blacksmith when I was twelve, with a knife.
> 5 Indians in self defence (behind a very safe rock).
> One man who bit me during a robbery.
> Brandy, Hindman, Beckwith, Joe Clark,
> Deputy Jim Carlyle, Deputy Sheriff J.W. Bell.
> And Bob Ollinger. A rabid cat
> birds during practice,
>
> These are the killed.
> (By them)
> Charlie, Tom O' Folliard
> Angela D's split arm,
> and Pat Garrett
> sliced off my head.
> Blood a necklace on me all my life.
>
> (*Collected Works*, 6)

Legend ascribes Billy at age 21 years and 21 victims while Ondaatje's Billy claims only 20 and is a little over 21 years by the time he dies. Numbers and figures, dates and years bring in an air of authenticity and with legendary figures like Billy, they have a special function to perform. Billy's age matches the number of his victims and he gets his first victim at the age of 12 that again is a reversal of 21. Most of the writers could not resist the temptation of numbers and figures and give in to the easy opportunity of mystifying the figures like Billy thereby indicating inexorable fate at work in the deeds and the destiny of the protagonist.

Ondaatje deploys the techniques of the earlier writers to unsettle their standard renderings of the legend. By ascribing Billy one victim less than the usual number Ondaatje refuses to be trapped in by the standard assumptions and does away with the simplistic attempts to seek an air authenticity and awe through a mechanical evoking of the supposed authority of numbers and figures. Billy's voice, his matter-of-fact balance sheet of the murders and the inclusion of even a 'rabid cat' and 'birds during practice' in the list of the killed ironically lend Ondaatje's description a greater air of authenticity although this is not what Ondaatje seeks. Even in his own creation of the image of Billy, Ondaatje is careful enough to avoid getting into any permanent fixtures. The *list of the killed* by Billy doesn't come to an end it stops short on a coma, thereby, leaving a number of possibilities open, perhaps Billy simply forgets to mention one or two earlier murders or commits some more after the enlistment or wants to keep the opportunity open for himself or in between his list, his mind wanders off to those killed by the others. While on the other hand the *list of the killed by the others* ends with a full stop and is apparently complete. But even here Billy himself is the last victim that again has significant implications.

By letting Billy speak about his own death and to include himself in the list of the killed Ondaatje on one hand indicates, as Scobie observes, his 'poetic assumption' of Billy's voice thereby stopping short the reader from getting carried away too far to believe the work to be Billy's own or the writer's attempt to produce such an impression while on the other hand Billy's inclusion of himself in the list may also be the possible result of his awareness of his destiny, his death at the hands of Pat Garrett.

Another minor detail about Billy in Ondaatje's source material, *The Saga of Billy Kid* by Burns is that Billy was left-handed although all the contemporary authorities describe Billy as right-handed. The idea of his being left-handed originated from the reversed image of one of his famous photographs. Though Burns mentions Billy as left-handed he does not go beyond this. Ondaatje shows a clear artistic preference for Billy's left-handedness because as Stephen Scobie remarks, "his left-handedness fits in better with the legendary image of the outsider" (*Poets and Critics*, 231). Ondaatje presents an intensely realised portrait of Billy's left-handedness that assumes almost mystic proportions as Garrett observes Billy:

> Bonney seemed relaxed and dressed very well, his left heel resting on his right knee. He ate corn, drank coffee, used a fork and knife alternately – always with his right hand. The three days we were together and at other times in our lives when we saw each other, he never used his left hand for anything except of course to shoot. He wouldn't even pick up a mug of coffee. I saw the hand, it was virgin white. Later when we talked about it, I explained about how a hand or muscle unused for much work would atrophy, grow small. He said he did fingers exercises subconsciously on the average 12 hours a day. And it was true. From then on I noticed his left hand churning within itself, each finger circling alternately like a train wheel. Curling into balls, pouring like waves across a tablecloth. It was the most hypnotizing beautiful thing I ever saw.
>
> (*Collected Works*, 43)

The vividness of the image, and the intricacy of the details transform Billy's left-handedness from an additional ability to an integral trait of his being. Being left-handed is being different, the earlier words for the trait being 'sinister' and 'gauche,' which now signify evil, awkwardness, clumsiness. Billy's left-handedness, in Scobie's opinion, confirms his Romantic image, alienates him further as an Outlaw/Outsider/Artist. Historical Billy was right-handed and the legendary left-handed. Ondaatje subtly transgresses both history and legend and makes Billy ambidextrous, with a 'virgin white' left hand reserved exclusively for shooting. Billy's deliberate use of the right hand for everything else, his grotesque, finger exercises maintain a delicate balance between the conscious and the subconscious. They speak of a violence that emerges from within and is beyond control 'churning within itself' like Billy's left hand. Billy appears enigmatic but brilliantly convincing. History and legend blend with Ondaatje's artistic, imaginative force and Billy the Kid's left-handedness is transferred into a mythical context.

A major difference between Ondaatje's approach and that of the earlier writers on the subject is the emphasis laid on assigning a motive to Billy the Kid's violence. The earlier writers depending on their fixation with the Saintly Billy or the Satanic Billy tried to find motives that varied from simple villainy to deceit, insulted honour, self-defense, and protection of friends. Ondaatje, on the other hand does not try to assign any easy motives to the surrounding violence. His Billy wonders in the book:

> A motive? some reasoning we can give to explain all this violence.
> Was there a source for all this? yup
>
> (*Collected Works*, 54)

By denying motives to Billy's violence Ondaatje makes himself and his Billy non-committal to any black or white portrayals of Billy. However denying a motive does not rule out the excessive violence of the era or the murders committed by Billy and by those who happened to be on the other side.

Ondaatje's Billy plays a substantial role in the upsurge of violence but far greater than his violent acts is the violence that exists within him. Billy is tormented by it in an intense subjective manner; in fact his perception is overridden with this violence narrowing down its circle on him:

> The others, I know did not see the wounds appearing in the sky, in the air. Sometimes a normal forehead in front of me leaked brain gasses. Once a nose clogged right before me, a lock of skin formed over the nostrils, and the shocked face had to start breathing through mouth, but then the mustache bound itself in the lower teeth and he began to gasp loud the hah! hah! Going strong – churned onto the floor, collapsed out, seeming in the end to be breathing out of his eye – tiny needle jets of air reaching into the throat. I told no one. If Angela D. had been with me then, not even her; not Sallie, John, Charlie, or Pat. In the end the only thing that never changed, never became deformed, were animals.
>
> (*Collected Works*, 10)

The above details endow Billy with a hallucinatory perception that probably has its roots in the deep penetration of the persecution complex into Billy's psyche. Ondaatje's Billy is locked within the tentacles of his violent perception and his acts of violence, at one level, his violence can be seen as his attempt to break himself free from the trap that persistently appears to suck him in. Ondaatje's Billy rather than revelling in the banging noise of bullets and the fall of his victims is escaping them. Billy is obsessed by the violence that occurs around him, things getting deformed, turning grotesque in the trap of death and is victimised by its hallucinatory manifestations in his subjective self. Billy's acute sensitivity towards his own self and his surroundings comes close to a psychopathological disorder. As he sees the world everything appears to be balanced too precariously always on the edge, on the verge of losing control and turning manic. Billy is persistently haunted by the delicate balance that exists between order and complete chaos:

> I have seen pictures of great stars,
> drawings which show them straining to the center
> that would explode their white
> if the temperature and speed they moved at shifted one degree.
>
> Or in the East have seen
> the dark grey yards where trains are fitted
> and the clean speed of machines
> that make machines, their
> red golden pouring which when cooled
> mists out to rust or grey.
>
> The beautiful machines pivoting on themselves
> sealing and fusing to others
> and men throwing levers like coins at them.
> And there is the same stress as with stars,
> the one altered move that will make them maniac.
>
> (*Collected Works*, 41)

There are multiple instances in the book that present Billy closely observing the horrifying metamorphosis of humans and animals into utter chaos. Billy, even in moments of absolute peace is overridden with the fear of this *one altered move* that will make them maniac. Ondaatje presents Billy taking shelter in a deserted barn to 'burn out his fever.' Though deserted, the barn is not without life, there are birds, insects, spiders and mice and Billy during his stay in the barn establishes a relationship of mutual acceptance with them:

> We were all aware and allowed each other. The fly who sat on my arm, after his inquiry, just went away, ate his disease and kept it in him. When I walked I avoided the cobwebs who had places to grow to, who had stories to finish. The flies caught in those acrobat nets were the only murder I saw.
>
> (*Collected Works*, 17)

However, this peace and harmony does not continue for long. Billy soon sees things turning *maniac* as a rain shower bursts power into the seeds in the granary. The rats that had earlier been eating the fermenting grain suddenly get drunk with the impact of the rain and:

> ... they abandoned the sanity of eating the food before them and turned on each other and grotesque and awkwardly because of their size they went for each other's eyes and ribs so the yellow stomachs slid out and they came through the door and killed a chipmunk – about ten of them onto that one striped thing and the ten eating each other before they realized the chipmunk was long gone ..... .
>
> (*Collected Works*, 18)

Ondaatje provides Billy's obsessive perception a realistic ground by closely following the experience of peace and harmony with a sudden production of chaos as nature makes *one altered move* turning the rats into horrible beasts. Billy is tormented by this constantly blurring margin between sanity and insanity, order and chaos. As with nature, animals and machines the human beings too are precariously balanced. In the story that John Chisum tells Billy and the others about Livingstone who bred a breed of mad dogs, there is almost a schizophrenic simultaneous coexistence of sanity and insanity. This man who used to sing with John and 'seemed a pretty sane guy' to him back home had been 'clinically and scientifically' inbreeding the dogs 'the worst with the worst' until they were reduced to 'heaps of bone and hair and sexual organs and bulging eyes and minds which were chaotic half out of hunger out of liquor out of their minds being pressed out of shape by new freakish bones that grew into their skulls' (*Collected Works*, 60–61).

These animals, if they could be called so, ultimately turn on to their master and eat him up. This story might be completely imaginary but in the book it has a context in Billy's world. What makes it all the more terrifying is the fact that Livingstone did not betray any visible signs of madness as if, as John sees it, 'he left all his madness, all his perverse logic, behind that fence on his farm and was washed pure by the time he came to town every Thursday' (61). The story may further confirm Billy's fears but it can have a seriously disconcerting effect even on those who do not possess Billy's perception. As Sallie who had been listening to the story whispers into the ear of her dog Henry – *Aint that a nasty story Henry, aint it? Aint it nasty* (62) – as if a nod from the dog might bring back her faith in him.

As with guns and violence yet another fundamental feature of the legends of outlaws is the hyperbolical presentation of their sexual prowess and exploits. The popular imagination loves to see the rugged hero taking a break from his saddle and guns to take, though temporary, a passionate plunge into love and lovemaking. Here too the hero has to give an incredible performance to carry his legend forward. From guns in the streets to women in bed he has to dominate with a characteristic ease making his *victims* gasp with disbelief. Ondaatje's Billy, however, is not seen as too good or too bad in bed but his experience of sex carries a virtual similarity with his hallucinatory perception of violence. Even in the act of lovemaking Billy is obsessed with a fear of being trapped. In the poem for Angela D Billy finds himself in such a position:

> ... she hooks in two and covers me
> my hand locked
> her body nearly breaking off my fingers
> pivoting like machines in final speed
> later my hands cracked in love juice
> fingers paralysed by its arthritic
> these beautiful fingers I couldn't move
> faster than a crippled witch now
>
> (*Collected Works*, 16)

In almost all the love scenes presented by Ondaatje, Billy faces this entrapment. In a song that Billy supposedly sings on a public platform for Angela Dickinson, he speaks out his mind:

> Her mouth is an outlaw
> she swallow your breath
> a thigh it can drown you
> or break off your neck
>
> Her throat is a kitchen
> red food and old heat
> her ears are a harp
> you tongue till it hurt
>
> Her toes take your ribs
> her fingers your mind
> her turns a gorilla
> to swallow you blind

(*Collected Works*, 64)

Both violence and sex elicit a similar response from Billy. Ondaatje's Billy is not a pattern of random acts, a loose gunslinger who went on shooting others until he himself was shot neither is he a murderer with a 'rightful' cause but beneath his enigma he is a thoroughly integrated character whose acts have their roots in and are governed by his perception of the world. Billy's obsessive consciousness of violence and sex as modes of imprisonment/destruction find an expression in the poem:

> The eyes bright scales
> (watch) bullet claws coming
> at me like women fingers
> part my hair slow
> go in slow in slow
> leaving skin in a puff
> behind and the slow
> as if fire pours out
> red grey brain the hair slow
> startled by it all pour

(*Collected Works*, 73)

The difference between the approach of a bullet and a woman stands at the minimal, bullet melts into a woman and the woman becomes a bullet to choke Billy as he pleads for life. The mingling of the two puts Billy into a consistently narrowing vicious circle that is sure to get him.. Billy constantly imagines himself in such a position and even exercises his fear on others. At one place he shoots a 'crooked' bird and as he holds it in his hands the bird 'shouts like trumpet' and Billy in turn 'destroys it of its fear.' Similarly in the poem on his birthday he does the same to the flies:

> catching flies with my left hand
> bringing the fist to my ear
> hearing the scream grey buzz
> as their legs cramp their
> heads with no air
> so eyes split and release
>
> (*Collected Works*, 58)

Ondaatje's image of Billy is a subtle rejection of all the earlier versions. Ondaatje attempts to touch the raw nerve of Billy's character and in doing so he discreetly distances himself from the historical or legendry Billy. Ondaatje's transformation of Billy into a myth, a phenomenon involves a looking into the vulnerability of Billy as a character in a certain situation.

Ondaatje shows a keen awareness of the narrow margin that exists between history and myth. While history derives all its strength and authority from its pretense of factual accuracy, myth by going beyond the authenticating tools of history, in its essential looseness captures the recurring patterns of the complex dialectics of human action and aspiration. It may appear paradoxical but myths have a greater credibility and influence than any substantiated historical chronicles. Myths come closer to truth of character as they apprehend the essence of character rather than concentrating on the upper crust of historical data.

History compromises itself to its strenuous linear accumulation of information and as a result is caught up in a deadlock, a rigidity that persists. Myths are fluid, liquid in character as they push the factual accuracy to the backdrop usurping the obvious claims of time and space and creating a dialectic that is at once temporal and timeless, spatial and spaceless.

Ondaatje's rejection of historical bias enables him to assume Billy's skin and voice and thus Ondaatje's claim is bigger than any of the preceding historical works on Billy. The real Billy might have been the hunter or the hunted, thoroughly wicked or kind hearted or one who never bothered himself to interpret his actions. Ondaatje's Billy is contradictorily tormented by his perception of violence, a possibility that none of the historical approaches considered worth exploring. The subjective self of Billy lies outside the trajectory of history and Ondaatje chooses this unexplored realm and provides even the most random and enigmatic acts of both historical and his own Billy with a psychologically rational context. A major part of the book deals with the subjective self of Billy and his objective exploits that won him the historical/legendry status remain in the backdrop and even when they are mentioned they are seen through the context of inward responses of Billy.

Central to Ondaatje's creation of the myth of Billy the Kid is his treatment of Garrett's character. Stephen Scobie notices how the reputation of Garrett has moved along with Billy (*Poets and Critics*, 241). If in the earlier versions Billy was satanic, Garrett occupied the opposite extreme of being an upright person and the trend reversed with favourable portrayals of Billy. Historically, the conflict between Billy and Garrett had economic reasons but as it is carried out in the book it finds its roots in the psyches of Billy and Garrett. Ondaatje makes it a conflict between mechanical neutrality of Garrett and Billy's vulnerability. Both Billy and Garrett are a perfect match for each other as far as their skills with guns are concerned. The vital difference lies in their ability to control chaos. Billy strives for a mechanical poise and cannot achieve it and Garrett has the upper hand as he has taught himself to be 'that rare thing – a sane assassin':

> Pat Garrett, ideal assassin. Public figure, the mind of a doctor, his hands hairy, scarred, burned by rope, on his wrist there was a purple stain there all his life. Ideal assassin for his mind was unwarped. Had the ability to kill someone on the street walk back and finish a joke. One who had decided what was right and forgot all morals.
>
> (*Collected Works*, 28)

There are two instances that consolidate Garrett's image of being *that rare thing the sane assassin*. In the shootings of Tom O' Folliard (7–8) and Charlie Bowdre (22); Garrett stands unmoved as his victims take their final walk towards him. While Billy has to avert his eyes as his victims collapse:

one must eliminate much
that is one turns when the bullet leaves you
walk off see none of the thrashing
the very eyes welling up like bad drains
believing then the moral of newspaper or gun
where bodies are mindless as paper you don't feed
or give to drink
that is why I can watch the stomach of clocks
shift their wheels and pins into each other
and emerge living, for hours

(*Collected Works*, 10)

Billy's perception makes him an underdog escaping the cold mechanical eliminating device, Pat Garrett. Ondaatje makes an interesting use of the term 'sane' in the context of Billy and Garrett. While Billy with his hallucinatory perception appears to be 'insane' and Garrett with his poise appears 'sane' and comes to chaos neutral, yet the apparent insanity of Billy is more human than Garrett's mechanical manoeuvres. The borders blur between sanity and insanity as Ondaatje puts them in an interesting order: *a sane assassin sane assassin sane assassin sane assassin sane assassin sane* (29). The 'in' at the end of assassin persistently gets into the succeeding sane making it 'insane' if read in rapid succession. Ondaatje pitches a vulnerable assassin Billy against a sane/insane machine and Billy is bound to lose this unequal struggle but even as he loses it he has the sympathy of the readers as Billy like the readers can apprehend the inevitable yet he braces himself to meet it headlong:

Garrett? I aint love-worn
torn aint blue I'm waiting
smelling you across the room
to kill you Garrett going

to take you from the knee up
leave me my dark AMATEUR!

(*Collected Works*, 53)

Ondaatje transforms Billy into a myth by converting the conflict between Billy and Garret into an inexorable pattern of struggle between human palpability and mechanical control. Garrett systematically eliminates the human in himself while Billy is tormented by it and every time he has to strive for a Garrett like control. The idea of death at the hands of Garrett looms large over Billy's imagination, howsoever slow Billy knows that Garrett is going to catch up with him. Billy is persistently haunted by the idea of his own death that it becomes a recurring aesthetic image, something that does not have the horror of death associated with it. In the list of the killed (by them) Billy includes himself:

and Pat Garrett
sliced off my head.
Blood a necklace on me all my life.

(*Collected Works*, 6)

Billy constantly imagines Garrett coming to him to get him. Billy imagines the path that Garrett's bullet will take into him and even as he dies he sees Garrett's jaw and stomach above himself, Ondaatje converts Billy's death into a poetic image.

Ondaatje's myth making is an intensely realised and carefully organised process. Apparently his technique comes close to the technique of collage making where a number of pictures are put together at random without a preconceived intention of producing a particular meaning or impression. Once the random images come together, the meaning/s emerging from the perspectives of the collage is looked upon making the collage fluid in nature. Though Billy the Kid may produce a similar impression, Ondaatje's presentation of his material is not a random act. The apparent randomness of his material is the result of an art that conceals art, though Ondaatje throws hints in his works that declare its entity as an artistic artifice. However, the result that he produces is amazingly realistic, as if moments, situations and characters have been caught in transit before they are transfixed into a particular image or melt into nothingness.

Ondaatje uses the different sources, approaches and the varied media that produce and emphasise a particular meaning or affix a certain image of a character. In Billy's case there is the establishmentarian history, the legend of the outlaw in popular imagination fostered by quasi-historical novelistic renderings and the movie westerns, the contemporary newspaper reports and accounts of the people who were supposedly close to Billy or were the eye-witnesses of some of his deeds and then there is the transformation of Billy into a comic book hero. Ondaatje draws from all these sources that claim to capture Billy and intersperses them between his own renderings of the legend.

In the acknowledgement section of the book Ondaatje makes the claim, "With these basic sources, I have edited, rephrased, and slightly reworked the originals. But the emotions belong to their authors." However, in view of the work the author's statement demand multiple readings. While on one hand the statement can be read as Ondaatje's humble acknowledgement of what he owes to the others but at the same time by making the assertion Ondaatje neatly distances himself from whatsoever impressions these sources might produce in their own right. By letting *the emotions belong to their authors* Ondaatje transfers the responsibility on the authors themselves saving himself from sharing the burden of interpretation and any attempt of narrow identification of his own approach with them.

Ondaatje allows the emotions to belong to their authors but as he uses these sources and *edits, rephrases and slightly reworks* the originals, the original texture of the emotions is drastically unsettled in their new contextualisation. Intertextuality in Ondaatje is not merely an act of promptly accredited scholarly borrowing but is rather an act of artistic appropriation. Even if Ondaatje quotes a source material unaltered he alters it by positioning it in a specific place within his work, introducing it unawares into an unexpected company forging hitherto unestablished relationships leading to newer meanings and implications. For instance, Ondaatje makes Billy wonder about the motive of excessive violence of his era and leaving a little gap on the page, follows it up with the account of Tunstall's murder (54) from Walter Noble Burns' *The Saga of Billy the Kid*. Burns lays emphasis on the brutality of the murderers and their 'devil's mockery' of laying Tunstall's body beside the dead horse so 'murdered man and dead horse suggested they had crawled into bed and gone to sleep together' (54). While Burns uses the account to establish the cruelty of Billy's opposite faction, Ondaatje by preceding it with Billy's 'yup' transforms the meaninglessness of this violence into a universal phenomenon where Billy is as active a perpetrator as those in the opposite faction.

Similarly, Ondaatje presents Miss Sallie Chisum's impressions of Billy and Garrett. While Sallie found Billy dressed as if 'he had just stepped out of a bandbox,' and 'a courteous little gentleman' (87). This goes against the image of Billy as being rough and roguish. Sallie's impression is preceded by the account of Billy's escape from the jail, his murders of Bell and Ollinger and the way he made his 'horse walk over Ollinger's body and went' (86). The juxtaposition of the two accounts captures contradictory images of Billy. On the two pages that follow Ondaatje first presents within parenthesis Garrett's love of stuffed birds (88) and follows it with Miss Chisum's opinion who found Garrett 'a remarkably handsome man' and in her final thoughts on Billy and Garrett has to say:

> I knew both these men intimately.
> There was good mixed in with the bad
> in Billy the Kid
> and bad mixed in with the good
> in Pat Garrett ...
>
> (*Collected Works*, 89)

Miss Sallie's opinion on the composition of Billy and Garrett is seriously undermined by the context in which Ondaatje puts it. Ondaatje's interventions make the characters of Billy and Garrett more complex than the simple formulation *good mixed with the bad* and *bad mixed with the good* might suggest. They resist easy reducibility and the images of Billy and Garrett from the perspective of the goodness or badness they might have possessed, remain absolutely partial, revealing only one aspect of these characters at a given moment. This is not to suggest that every time Ondaatje uses his source material to undermine it because at times the source material reinforces an Ondaatjean image but the author takes care not to take any of the details too far neither his own nor that of the others. His process is that of constant checks through interventions and impositions, a pattern of simultaneous construction and dismantling. The process enables Ondaatje to preserve an openness that allows space to the characters and leaves room for constant negotiations in terms of meanings and implications.

Ondaatje's myth making also involves an appropriation of the corresponding techniques of his source material. The legend of Billy the Kid has been established through varied means of photography, history, novels, movies and comic books and each of these mediums claim to capture the 'truth' of Billy's character. Ondaatje internalises the techniques of these mediums to suit his own purposes. It allows Ondaatje to look at Billy through them and at the same time to look through the processes themselves. Ondaatje's inclusion and assimilation of these processes into his own approach emphasises their insuperable association with the legend of Billy the Kid.

Photographs play a crucial role in establishing and providing an air of authenticity to characters grounded in history. Ondaatje makes an interesting use of photographs and the technique of photography in his book. He uses nine photographs in the book and ironically none of the photographs shows Billy. These photographs appear to be randomly selected and interspersed in the book though they are not arbitrary any manner. Ondaatje's choice is deliberate as he leaves out the photographs of Billy, Garrett or the others and even the places that are historically associated with Billy.

Ondaatje's photographs apparently approach Billy and his world from the periphery but they have central significance in Ondaatje's creation of the myth of Billy the Kid. Two of them are the photographs of drawings. In one a man opens a door and finds himself in a room full of snakes and dead men, in the other a beautiful woman sits on a lavish bed in a seductive posture.

Ondaatje places the first picture after Billy has a night of excessive drinking and the subsequent throwing up with the Chisums, Angela D. and Garrett (68) and the image is followed by the account of Billy waking up in the morning. The picture occupies the intervening space between the accounts of the night and the morning indicating a possible nightmare that Billy might have had. The second picture is placed after Billy's song for Angela D. (64) and has a different narrative implication. The image acquires a complex depth as the juxtaposition of the song with the image brings out the deceptive nature of an inviting seductive gesture, the potential threat that may 'swallow you blind' (64).

Both the pictures have a psychological basis in Billy's world, they can be seen as the manifestations of Billy's obsession with the ideas of chaos and seduction. Then there are two photographs in which the characters are on the verge of walking out of the frames:

The first photograph appears after the poems that present the image of Charlie's horrifying death and the image of a 'headless hen jerking brown all the yard' (12). Ondaatje, in place of presenting a violent image in the photograph depicts what appears like a lawman leaving, walking out of the frame, out of action, a complete contrast to the violence of the preceding images. The second photograph of a dog with his master in the cart presents an image of harmony, a bleak anticipation of what may follow. But there is a complete reversal of any such anticipation as Ondaatje follows it up with the horrifying tale of Livingstone breeding dogs into madness (60). On the level of technique, characters moving out of the frame bring out the curious nature of 'truth' in representation, the medium vis-à-vis life where life always seems to be moving out of the frame, resisting restriction into a static image.

All these photographs have complex thematic implications and are closely linked to the narrative regulating its movement through contrasts, reemphasis, sudden interjections and anticipations. However, Ondaatje draws even more from the technique of photography in his narrative. A considerable part of his narrative is photographic in nature and the book can be seen as an album of verbal photographs alongside the visual ones. Billy often looks at his surroundings as if from the eyes of a camera and in his subjective moods appears to turn the camera inwards. In one of the poems Ondaatje projects Billy waiting for friends or enemies:

I am here on the edge of sun
that would ignite me
looking into pitch white
sky and grass overdeveloped to meaninglessness
waiting for enemies' friends or mine

(*Collected Works*, 74)

In another poem Billy looks into his senses with the eye of a camera:

I am here with the range for everything
corpuscle muscle hair
hands that need the rub of metal
those senses
that want to crash things with an axe
that listen to deep buried veins in our palms … .

(*Collected Works*, 72)

As Billy lies on bed and sees Angela D. approaching him he resembles a photographer carefully positioning himself to capture an image with all the intricacies of light and darkness:

She walks slow to the window
lifts the sackcloth
and jams it horizontal on a nail
so the bent oblong of sun
hoists itself across the room
framing the bed the white flesh
of my arm …
I am very still
I take in all the angles of the room

(*Collected Works*, 21)

The above examples are photographs in words. Ondaatje's technique establishes interesting parallels between an outlaw's and a photographer's perspective of the world around them. Both 'aim' and 'shoot' considering the angles available to them. At one level Ondaatje himself becomes a photographer trying to capture Billy from the different angles. However, Ondaatje's adoption of photographic technique in his work is ostensibly the outcome of his awareness of the role of photographs in establishing the cowboy legend. The cowboys and outlaws including Billy were extremely fond of posing for photographs and had their fanciful notions of dressing themselves in specific clothes, alongside the guns and in particular posture that presumably brought out their menacing or romantic best depending on the mood or the impression they wanted to create.

Ondaatje is precisely aware of the gap that exists between a pose and the revealing moments that precede the made up impression and also of the fact that there are things outside the focus of the camera and life moves while a camera captures an image in stasis. The photographs that Ondaatje uses are not exactly photographs in the general sense, as rather than presenting a construed image they reflect the limitations of the medium itself.

In the beginning of the book in place of presenting the commonly used photograph of Billy, Ondaatje presents an empty frame and just below it quotes the frontier photographer L.A. Huffman's comment that claims the photograph to be that of Billy. A few pages later Paulita Maxwell's opinion of the photograph appears:

> In 1880 a travelling photographer came through Fort Sumner. Billy posed standing in the street near old Beaver Smith's saloon. The picture makes him look rough and uncouth.
>
> The expression of his face was really boyish and pleasant. He may have worn such clothes as appear in the picture out on the range, but in Sumner he was careful of his personal appearance and dressed neatly and in good taste. I never liked the picture. I don't think it does Billy justice.

(*Collected Works*, 19)

The comments of Huffman and Paulita Maxwell apparently contradict each other. While Huffman is quite certain of capturing Billy in his photograph, Paulita Maxwell finds the photograph not doing *justice* to Billy. As far as the *justice* of her own impression is concerned Ondaatje follows her comment by making Billy speak:

> Not a story about me through their eyes then. Find the beginning, the slight silver key to unlock it, to dig it out. Here then is a maze to begin, be in.
>
> (*Collected Works*, 20)

Ondaatje's juxtaposition of the two comments alongside his own insertions, makes each of the comments self-reflexive thereby emphasising the partial nature of the representation of the truth of Billy's character through each medium whether photography or personal impressions. As for himself Ondaatje chooses an empty frame and at the end of the book the frame presents Ondaatje himself as a boy in an outlaw outfit in one corner. Ondaatje disclaims the notion of absolute truth in representation whether artistic or otherwise. By inserting his own photograph in one corner of an empty, frame Ondaatje disclaims the truth of his portrait of Billy which remains largely personal and is at one level the manifestation of the Billy in his own self. It is Ondaatje as Billy and the emptiness of the remaining part of the frame reemphasises the partial nature of even the author as the subject.

Another strong element in the establishment of the legend of Billy the Kid is the role of movies. The cinematographic technique has a visible influence in the book. There are numerous instances that produce a cinematic effect. The scene in which Tom O' Folliard enters Sumner on the Christmas eve (7) and is shot by Garrett, is structured in a manner that it produces the impression of a graphic presentation of the characteristic scene from the western movies that presents the unsuspecting outlaw entering a town walking right into the middle of the trap that his ambushers have laid for him. Ondaatje does not limit the influence of the cinematographic technique to outward descriptions but as with photography the medium has a subjective influence in Billy's way of thinking:

> His stomach was warm
> remembered this when I put my hand into
> a pot of luke warm tea to wash it out
> dragging out the stomach to get the bullet
> he wanted to see when taking tea
> with Sallie Chisum in Paris Texas

With Sallie Chisum in Paris Texas
he wanted to see when taking tea
dragging out the stomach to get the bullet
a pot of luke warm tea to wash it out
remembered this when I put my hand into
his stomach was warm

(*Collected Works*, 27)

The order of the lines in the first stanza is inverted in the second and so is the image, in the manner of a slow motion sequence in a movie slowly getting back to the beginning. The inversion reinforces the image of the bullet in the stomach and the luke warm tea, the warmth the of stomach and the tea blending into one image in Billy's mind, catching him in a circle.

Ondaatje also uses flashbacks and flash-forwards in the manner of the movies. The shooting of Charlie at Tivan Arroyo by Garrett and the consequent arrest of Billy the Kid, Wilson and Dave Rudabaugh is not presented in the sequence that they occur (22). The poem on Charlie's death precedes this account and Ondaatje picks up the incident in a flashback much later (48) and this time he does not mention the death of Charlie but simply concentrates on the external details the corresponding positions of Garrett and his accomplices and Billy and his friends. The arrest is mentioned even farther into the narrative (76). The breaking of the narrative and the recurrence of the scene with the addition of new details each time emphasises the circular manner in which climactic occurrences keep coming back to Billy's mind. Similarly, Ondaatje deploys the technique of flash-forward in repeatedly anticipating Billy's death at the hands of Garrett:

Down the street was a dog. Some mut spaniel, black and white.

One dog, Garrett and two friends, stud looking, came down the street to the house, to me.

Again.
Down the street was a dog. Some mut spaniel, black and white.
One dog, Garrett and two friends came down the street to the house, to me.

> Garrett takes off his hat and leaves it outside the door. The others laugh. Garrett smiles, pokes his gun towards the door. The others melt and surround.
>
> All this I would have seen if I was on the roof looking.
>
> (*Collected Works*, 46)

The 'Again' in the above passage and the repeated lines except the detail about Garret's friends 'stud looking' produce an impression as if Billy replays the scene in his mind moments before his death imagining the approach of Garrett and his friends from the angle of the roof where he was not as they surrounded him. On the level of the narrative the sequence produces a foreboding impression of Billy's final entrapment. The image remaining at the back of the reader's mind as s/he proceeds further into the narrative. Moments after Billy is shot, Ondaatje presents the scene from *the screen of a horse's eye*:

> OUTSIDE
> the outline of horses
> Garrett running from a door
> – all seen sliding round
> the screen of a horse's eye
>
> (*Collected Works*, 94)

Ondaatje exploits the techniques of photography and cinematography to project Billy's world that alternates between stasis and kinesis, harmony and utter chaos, Billy remaining on the verge. The stills, slow motions, flashbacks and flash-forwards do not just influence the movement of the narrative but they are thoroughly integrated into Billy's character. Ondaatje's Billy is a product of the processes. By incorporating the processes into his creation of the myth of Billy the Kid, Ondaatje achieves multiple objectives. He projects these processes inextricably bound with the image of Billy, the limitations that they have and at the same time how a deeper exploitation of these mediums may release a figure like Billy the Kid from the standard, stereotypical determinations.

Ondaatje transforms the legend of Billy the Kid into a myth by trying not to capture or restrict Billy to a certain frame, precisely by allowing him to escape the different attempts to frame him. Rather than the legend itself, Ondaatje is more interested in exploring the processes the *when, where* and *how* of a character's metamorphosis into a myth. By concentrating on the processes that formulate a certain image of a character Ondaatje expostulates the fundamental fact that when a character is appropriated by any of the mediums of representation – history, legend, photography, journalistic interpretations, memoirs, novels or movies – it begins to have a life that runs independent of the real life of the character and is dominated by the nuances of the medium of representation.

A majority of these mediums insist on being 'truthful' and each claiming a greater reliability than the other modes of representation. The other mediums like movies and comic books dwell in the realm of imaginative recreations drawing upon certain characteristics of the subject and developing them to suit their purposes. Primarily, these representations oscillate between the factual and the imaginary but in either case they tend to transform the subject into a stereotype. For Ondaatje the mythical potential of a character lies somewhere between the rational and the purely imaginary, between the harmonious and the ambiguous. Ondaatje's treatment of Billy shows his acute awareness of the line of distinction between the stereotypes offered by the other mediums and the archetypes offered by the mythical mode.

Ondaatje creates the myth of Billy by emphasising the vulnerability and the construed nature of other modes of representation and attempts to free Billy from the confinement of his stereotypical image. While the real Billy the Kid might have been persecuted by Pat Garrett Ondaatje's Billy undergoes a double victimisation. On one side there is the sheriff and on the other there are history, legend, memoirs, movies, newspapers, comic books that persecute Billy and try to frame him. Ondaatje's Billy is not only escaping Pat Garrett but also the mediums that try to detain him within their clutches. The restlessness that Ondaatje himself might have felt in going through the manners in which Billy has been represented is transformed by him into an integral trait of Billy's character. Billy's fear of being trapped in life has an aesthetic value in Ondaatje's text as he allows Billy escape routes from the pressing attempts of stereotypic determinations. Garrett in the book sees the physical manifestation of Billy's fear:

> He would usually be hooked in ridiculous positions, feet locked in the chair's arms, or lying on the floor with his feet up. He could never remain in one position more than five minutes.
>
> (*Collected Works*, 43–44)

Ondaatje does not let Billy remain in one position for long in life as well as in the text. Ondaatje's Billy keeps escaping Garrett and the modes of determination.

One crucial aspect of the legend of Billy the Kid is the speculation that surrounds his death. The authors of the authentic versions of Billy's life are divided in their opinion regarding the death of Billy. While some try to establish that Garrett got Billy the others are of the opinion that Billy escaped with his Mexican sweet-heart and somebody else was killed in his place. Ondaatje quotes a piece of dialogue between Garrett and Poe from the account written by Deputy John W. Poe in 1919:

> *"It was the Kid who came in there to me," Garrett told Poe, "and I think I got him."*
>
> *"Pat," replied Poe, "I believe you have killed the wrong man."*
>
> *"I'm sure it was the Kid," responded Garrett, "for I knew his voice and could not have been mistaken."*
>
> (*Collected Works*, 103)

Ondaatje follows the account of Poe with a poem in which Garrett and the others seem to celebrate the death of Billy and as they clean up his body they discover something strange:

> We got the eight foot garden hose
> turned it on, leaned him down flat.
>
> What fell away we threw away
> his head was smaller than a rat.
>
> (*Collected Works*, 104)

The cleaning up of Billy leaves very little of him and his head is *smaller than a rat*. A large part of Billy disappears with water suggesting the disposability of the part. Below the surface of the legend Billy is reduced to nothingness. Ondaatje does not try to cash upon this standard trick but lets Billy escape in more complex ways than any of the authentic versions might suggest. Ondaatje's Billy escapes into a myth. While Pat Garrett might have captured the real Billy the Kid with a head smaller than a rat they could not get the mythical Billy that escaped with water and keeps escaping every time there is an attempt to trap him. Ondaatje imagines digging up the grave of Billy:

> Imagine if you dug him up and brought him out. You'd see very little. There'd be the buck teeth. Perhaps Garrett's bullet no longer in thick wet flesh would roll in the skull like a marble. From the head there'd be a trail of vertebrae like a row of pearl buttons off a rich coat down to the pelvis. The arms would be cramped on the edge of what was the box. And a pair of handcuffs holding ridiculously the fine ankle bones. (Even though dead they buried him in leg irons). There would be silver from the toe of each boot.
>
> His legend a jungle sleep
>
> (*Collected Works*, 97)

The seekers of 'real' Billy the Kid have to translate Billy from the pair of handcuffs around the fine anklebones, Garrett's bullet in his head and the silver from his boots. Ondaatje's Billy finds a life in myth that goes beyond his own life and his era and transforms him into an enigmatic and recurring pattern of the outlaw/artist/outsider/the other/the underdog challenging the forces greater than himself attempting to measure himself like Billy 'experimenting on how good you are'. For Ondaatje the legend of Billy remains *a jungle sleep* that from a distance may appear absolutely still but up close reveals life churning in countless voices and silences awaiting translation.

The myth of the Wild Wild West and the likes of Billy the Kid still goes on in the popular cinema of the west as well as other countries around the world. Hollywood has repeatedly returned to the west and the lore of the cowboy, there have been consistent historical renderings of the cowboy lore and film stars like Paul Newman and Clint Eastwood have played the cowboy so often that they have come to be inextricably attached to the image of the cowboy. Hollywood still sees the cowboy as the iconic symbol of unrestricted freedom, dominated by the moment, with little or no respect for law but undeniably generous, ready to lay down his life for friends. There have been movies that present the contemporary cowboy finding himself in the metropolis, playing havoc with the city and its manners, false sophistication, taking the entire city for a ride as he brings the badman to his fate, discovering love in the process but in the end deserting the city for the haven of the west.

In the context of the former colonies like India or Sri Lanka, the myth of the cowboy has played a significant role in the popular imagination. During the 40s as these countries were on the verge of the end of the colonial rule, this American myth offered them a welcome break from the oppressive hegemony of the British culture. The cowboy with his anti-establishment attitude and liberties he took with the manners and mannerisms of the genteel class, was an easy figure to relate to. In the case of the upper class and the bourgeois who had been educated like Michael Ondaatje strictly according to the traditions of British colonial education, the cowboy and his way of living was a source of relief, a figure to identify with. In the popular cinema in India the cowboy myth has merged with the myths of the bandits. Though a great number of movies have attempted to replicate the cowboy environ by presenting leather hats, horses, wooden structures, and saloons but the movies that have blended elements of the cowboy myth with the myth of the bandits, where the hero takes to horses and guns to face the villain in the wilderness have proved very successful.

The influence has not been one sided. The Asian myths, in the contemporary context, have made inroads into Hollywood and even into its romance with the cowboy myth. Some of the recent movies bring the cowboy in odd-pairings. In these movies the western outlaw finds himself, by pure coincidence, in the company of a Chinaman; the man on some mission of his own brings in all the wisdom of the East and the secrets of martial arts. There are sneering responses from the western outlaw in the beginning but the eventual discovery that the man is much more than the image of a Chinaman, has a great adaptability and may beat the cowboy at his own game. Such projections clearly reveal that the world has come to a stage where singular cultural, mythical projections have become obsolete and the cultures have to look for counterparts and blends thing from other cultures to retain their vitality.

Works Cited

Jewinski, Ed. *Express Yourself Beautifully*. ECW Press, 1998.

Ondaatje, Michael. *The Collected Works of Billy the Kid: Left Handed Poems*. London: Picador, 1981.

Polley, Jane. Ed. *The Reader's Digest Book of American Folklore and Legend*. ISBN, 1978.

Solecki, Sam. "Two Authors in Search of a Character: Michael Ondaatje and bpNichol", *Poets and Critics: Essays from Canadian Literature 1966–1974*. Ed. George Woodcock, Toronto: OUP 1974.

3

In Between Races and Places

The Challenge of Belonging

> After all Taormina, Ceylon, Africa, America – as far as *we* go, they are only the negations of what we ourselves stand for and are: and we're rather like Jonahs running away from the places we belong.
>
> ... Ceylon is an experience – but heavens not a permanence.
>
> D.H. Lawrence
> (qtd. by Ondaatje, *Running in the Family*, 78)

Lawrence's statement addresses certain key issues in postcolonial writing. The italicised 'we' draws a clear line of distinction between European civilisations and the rest of the world. It brings into focus the Eurocentric ideas of identity and the modes of perception that emphasise the difference between the two worlds; primarily, upon two levels – *what we stand for and are* – that is, the difference in terms of culture, religion, ethics and ethos beside the other more visible differences of race, colour, and locale. Lawrence might have been earnestly appalled by the Ceylonese natives, the excessive heat, rapidly changing weather and the noises of the Orient but these factors, somehow, did not restrain Europe from being pulled towards the Orient and the imposition of long centuries of exploitation under the eventual disguise of carrying and dislodging the 'white man's burden'.

However, Lawrence makes a significant point when he puts the European voyages in a mythical context – *we're rather like Jonahs running away from the places we belong* – a pattern that was to reverse; as with the advent of the twentieth century the world was to be full of *Jonahs* and this time from the other world; running away from the places they belonged to seek better opportunities, refuge and new homes; carrying with them their distinct cultures, the memories, the scars, real and imagined, of their colonial past right into the hearts of the ex-imperial centres.

The political and economic upheavals of the twentieth century exercised an unprecedented influence over the religious and socio-cultural domains of the world. The increased accessibility of geo-political spaces between the hitherto segregated worlds converted the world into a vast theatre of epic voyages with immigrants/refugees of economic, political and religious nature embarking upon individual exodus of their own. The twentieth century to a great extent was the era of immigration, which brought the people of different racial and ethnic origins into close proximity, juxtaposed the coloniser and the colonised, thereby bringing the given and inherent differences between them into sharper focus and making the questions of identity, roots, the notions of selfhood and otherness crucial to contemporary enquiry.

Michael Ondaatje's position in this context is an interesting and intriguing example of the complexity of the contemporary questions of identity. J.E. Chamberlin in his review of Ondaatje's poems has observed:

> Ondaatje is in a curious position as a poet, but a position that is close to that of other contemporary poets writing out of situations that define essentially colonial predicaments, where language or audience or the identity or the role of the poet are indeterminate ... Canada offers Ondaatje a geography but no inheritance; Sri Lanka offers him a family history, but no tradition, no way of passing things on; the English language offers him both an inheritance and a history, but no time and place.[1]

Chamberlin's remark captures the predicament of the expatriate writer, whereby the physical dislocation of the writer forces the geographical, socio-cultural belongings, the questions of history, inheritance, tradition and language into a complex relationship. A relationship that has to be negotiated afresh, but while Chamberlin appears to suggest a kind of 'lost world' situation for the expatriate writer, and apprehends an essential disadvantage in the indeterminate status of Ondaatje or that of the other contemporaries; it has to be acknowledged that the notions of history, inheritance, tradition and language are in themselves indeterminate, they evolve with inter-cultural influences and cannot be treated as 'givens'; something that can be carried or handed down through generations untainted, unaltered. The expatriate writers, through their physical and multiple dislocations/relocations experience the cross-cultural influences, are transformed by them as they transform the cultures and spaces they step in and step through.

Susan Spearey in "Mapping and Masking: The Migrant Experience in Michael Ondaatje's *In the Skin of a Lion*" observes, "By alluding to and reappropriating received stories, traditions and generic conventions, Ondaatje stakes his claim to a cross-cultural inheritance, and pieces together an alternative literary tradition that answers to his most pressing concerns as a migrant writer. Similarly, he shapes connections with old worlds and new, situating himself in relation to their various geographies and histories" (Spearey, 48). Appropriation, reappropriation and assimilation of diverse and discordant relationships have an important function in the expatriate experience; they work almost as imperatives and involve a certain amount of deliberation as the expatriate negotiates the contradictory claims and multiple pulls in his sense of being and belonging.

Michael Ondaatje has chosen subjects that are situated away from both Sri Lanka and Canada. *Collected Works of Billy the Kid* (1970) and *Coming Through Slaughter* (1976) are located in New Mexico and New Orleans respectively. Ondaatje enters the seemingly unrelated worlds of William Bonney, a legendary American outlaw and Buddy Bolden, an obscure black jazz musician, and transforms the outlaw, the artist and their corresponding worlds into a lived experience, providing them mythic dimensions. The roots of Ondaatje's choice of the two may well lie in his fascination for the popular western comics and movies that featured Billy while in the case of Buddy, his very obscurity and the deep involvement with his art that took away his sanity, a subject that concerns Ondaatje himself as an artist. Culturally, both Billy and Buddy are far from the worlds of Ondaatje yet they are manifested in Ondaatje's psyche in complex ways, strike some visible and hidden chords in him. Through them Ondaatje negotiates the other worlds that have no obvious connections with him.

Questions of identity, history, inheritance and belonging are crucial for the expatriate writers. *Running in the Family* (1982) and *In the Skin of a Lion* (1987) are the first books in which Ondaatje deals directly with the home of his inheritance and that of his adoption. The books are very different in nature and in the choice of genres, the first a concoction of a memoir, travelogue, poetry and intriguing fiction and the second is more close to the genre of the postmodern novel. In these two books Ondaatje negotiates the vastly different landscapes of Sri Lanka and Canada that converge and depart in subtle and violent ways in his psyche, sensibility and being. As Ondaatje explores these two spaces of his origin and of adoption, he brings into consideration history, memory, myth, culture and their claims upon individual identity. Different as the two books are, they have a strong common element, both the books in their own characteristic ways are narratives of belonging. A juxtaposition of the two reveals the challenges countered by the expatriate and the strong urge to feel comfortable within both the spaces with all their contradictions.

As the expatriate negotiates the opposing spaces of his origin and that of adoption, the strategies differ. The country of origin involves a looking back and there is a strong element of memory, both personal and communal. The cultural inheritance, and the past home is looked upon with nostalgia. Emotional ties, pain of separation surface and demand resolution. However, still greater is the challenge to seek a belonging with the country in the present with the distance of time and space. The treatment of the country of adoption involves an understanding of the landscape, culture, their internalisation to some extent and carving out a place in socio-economic and political terms. Multiple pulls, complex impulses, tug at/in the expatriate self as he/she struggles to negotiate identity and stability.

Ondaatje left Sri Lanka at the age of eleven, studied in England for eight years and migrated to Canada at the age of nineteen. Since then he has lived in Canada. His own experience of Sri Lanka is limited to the days of his childhood and the few journeys that he undertook to the island years later. As he took to the writing of *Running in the Family*, he was experiencing some moments of crises in his marital life and back home, in Sri Lanka, his father died. Michael had always known his father from a distance and as some of the very painful events took place, his father's increasing drunkenness and erratic behaviour and the gradual dissipation of his parent's marriage, Michael remained oblivious. He learnt about the moments that transformed his life only in his maturity.

The title of the book holds vital clues – it speaks of an urge to run in, to feel one with the family; it is also an attempt to understand what *runs* in the family in terms of attitudes, obsessions, virtues, vices, habits, strengths, weaknesses – the deep layers of a complex inheritance, that an individual carries within his self, in his genes that may often surprise him with their unexpected manifestations at different moments of his life. As mentioned earlier, memory plays a vital role in the treatment of the home space. Ondaatje's own memory of the island is limited to the faint or some scattered striking impressions or experiences of his childhood. In his attempt of running in the family, Ondaatje uses both personal memory as well as the recollections of his relatives, history both recorded and oral, stories told from different perspectives where the plot, events and consequences change with each narrator and are sometimes collectively agreed upon, archival sources, newspapers, photographs, engravings on stones and in the minds and hearts of those who have been through the tides of time. And as the book unfolds, all these sources, fictional or the more authentic ones, are rendered palpable, are caught up in a complex self-reflexivity induced by their strange juxtaposition. The only constant appears to be the Sri Lankan landscape in which 'Drive ten miles and you are in a landscape so different that by rights it should belong to another country' (147).

Even the most professed, discreet, and rooted attempts, with clearly discernible patterns, of the reclamation of past or an exploration of roots are acts of imaginative reconstruction. An act that cannot stand on one leg of factual accuracy of history with its linear, chronological, singular perspective; history itself being a construct, an artefact saying much less than what it carefully leaves out. Ondaatje expresses his restlessness with history in the book:

> Truth disappears with history and gossip tells us in the end nothing of personal relationship ... Individuals are seen only in the context of these swirling social tides ... Where is the intimate and truthful in all this? Teenager and uncle. Husband and lover. A lost father in his solace. And why do I want to know of this privacy? After the cups of tea, coffee, public conversation ... I want to sit down with someone and talk with utter directness, want to talk to all the lost history like that deserving lover. (53–54)

Both history and gossip are suspects. Each in its own way incomplete, revealing only partial truths, leaving out gaps that demand to be filled in. While Ondaatje desires utter directness, he knows that there cannot be one approach or perspective that may reveal the lost history with all its intimacy. Ondaatje's narrative reveals the vulnerability of each approach including his own. Ondaatje carefully depicts how history, memory, photographs from family albums, names, deeds and stories engraved on stones and in documents are constantly corroded; the corrosion almost an objective manifestation of their incompleteness. The nature of cognition and reality intervene.

As Ondaatje sits with his aunt discussing the history of good and bad Ondaatjes, the boundaries between history, story, rumour blur, each exposing the other. Ondaatje anticipates:

> In the heart of this 250–year-old fort we will trade anecdotes and faint memories, trying to swell them with the order of dates and asides, interlocking them all as if assembling the hull of a ship. No story is ever told just once. Whether a memory or funny hideous scandal, we will return to it an hour later and retell the story with additions and this time a few judgments thrown in. In this way history is organized. (26)

Ondaatje does not associate history with family but leaves it there alone, hinting invention, multiple intrusions in the way it is organised or should be organised. He mentions family photographs, the captured moments being eaten away by silverfish, the frozen opera of his parents' generation, the names on church stones worn out by visitors' feet, houses invaded by gardens, memory invading the present. His aunt Dolly who had almost lost her sight, shows him a photograph:

> She has looked at it for years and has in this way memorized everyone's place in the picture. She reels off names and laughs at the facial expressions she can no longer see. It has moved tangible, palpable, into her brain, the way memory invades the present in those who are old, the way the gardens invade houses here, the way her tiny body steps into mine as intimate as anything I have witnessed and I have to force myself to be gentle with this frailty in the midst of my embrace. (112)

There is a feeling of fleeting moments, truth and history determined to escape, to disintegrate with all the efforts to restrain or control them. Ondaatje is aware of the evasive nature of his own task, the impossibility of determination as he struggles to bring and hold together the different threads of the story. At one moment in the story, the barriers between the searcher and the searched, Ondaatje and his father, collapse, the moment of absolute identification with the other. As the narrative moves it is difficult to distinguish one from the other:

> In the bathroom the ants had attacked the novel thrown on the floor by the commode. A whole battalion was carrying one page away from its source, carrying the intimate print as if rolling a tablet away from him. He knelt down on the red tile, slowly not wishing to disturb their work. It was page 189. He had not got that far in the book yet but he surrendered it to them. (189)

Ondaatje, as he moves towards capturing the family history with all its intimacies, is aware that it eludes him even before he gets there, something that makes him 'scared by the company of the mirror' (189), to be framed in the certainty of the mirror, while everything else disintegrates in and around him. Even as history disintegrates, memory eludes and gossip evaporates, they reveal a pattern of relationships, of belonging in their intricate interwoven threads as beautiful and fascinating as the patterns of colours in the

Sri Lankan sarongs. Ondaatje approaches Sri Lanka with multiple perspectives, picking the character of the island, his family, the historical and contemporary relationships, and tries to capture his own place both historically and the way he wishes to relate to the fabric of Ceylon in all its vividness.

Running in the Family has several layers of conception and execution. The work, complex as it is, can be read from several perspectives but what transpires through all its complexities is the writer's grappling with the issue of otherness; not only at an individualistic level but the otherness he attempts to comprehend and comes to terms with is the otherness of an entire community, the Burghers, with native and European blood in their veins and a history of five centuries in the Sri Lankan landscape. The Burghers have an interesting history in Ceylon. Originally, the term was the Dutch word for adventure seekers who went to places like Capetown, Borneo and Ceylon. Later on in Ceylon, the term came to signify the community that developed as a result of the intermarriages between the Dutch and the natives.[2]

Ondaatje presents a beautiful account, in *Running in the Family*, of how Ceylon enticed the invaders, traders, and adventure seekers alike, some of whom settled on the island and others who left taking their plunder along with them, but they all left a distinct mark on Ceylonese history, society and culture which evolved with its name:

> The island seduced all Europe. The Portugese. The Dutch. The English. And so its name changed, as well as its shape – Serendip, Ratnapida ("island of gems"), Taprobane, Zeloan, Zeilan, Seyllan, Ceilon, and Ceylon – the wife of many marriages, courted by invaders who stepped ashore and claimed everything with the power of sword or bible or language. (64)

The Burghers are the genuine progeny of this *wife of many marriages*. In them could be seen the culmination of the best and in some cases the worst of both the worlds. They appropriated the power of the invaders' 'sword', 'bible' and 'language' and also the knowledge and lineage of the natives. Though the Burghers have spent almost six centuries in Ceylon, a long enough time to call a place home, and they were essentially the elite for more than five centuries in the Ceylonese society yet, with their hybridity they always stood in the margins between nativity and foreignness; eagerly identifying with one or the other, or with both, or refusing both and inverting upon themselves converting their existence into a literal island within the island.

The hybridity and the inherent ambivalence of the Burghers are well brought out in *Running in the Family* by Ondaatje. Ondaatje observes the curious nature of relationships:

> This was Nuwara Eliya in the twenties and the thirties. Everyone was vaguely related and had Sinhalese, Tamil, Dutch, British and Burgher blood in them going back many generations. There was a large social gap between this circle and the Europeans and the English who were never a part of the Ceylonese community. The English were seen as transients, snobs and racists, and were quite separate from those who had intermarried and lived here permanently. (41)

This curious hybrid group of people might not consider the British a part of the Ceylonese community, but they themselves are almost an alienated group with narrow boundaries of their own that separated them from the larger Ceylonese community. While they considered the English 'transients, snobs and racists', they had predominantly English inclinations in education, language, clothes and intellectual pursuits. Ondaatje's grandfather, father, uncle, aunts, other relatives and Ondaatje himself took the voyages to England as a natural sequel to their British colonial education in Ceylon. The examples of their affinity to the British abound in the book. Ondaatje's grandfather, Bampa, he mentions in the book, visited England every two years bought crystal and learnt latest dances. He maintained a strict tradition of kissing each other good night and good morning in the family:

> Like some other Ondaatjes, Bampa had a weakness for pretending to be 'English' and, in his starched collars and gray suits, was determined in his customs. My brother, who was only four years old then, still remembers painfully strict meals at Rock Hill with Bampa grinding his teeth at one end of the table – as if his carefully built ceremonies were being evaded by a weak-willed family. It was only in the afternoons when he dressed in sarong and vest ... that he seemed to become a real part of the landscape around him. (56)

The weakness for pretending to be English is not an eccentric trait limited to the Ondaatjes. In it can be seen the typical trait of the colonised to imitate the masters. But in the case of Burghers it is slightly different because their imitation of the British conveys a sense of authority in the appropriation of British manners, which is very different from the meekish, self-conscious assumption of the masters' manners by the natives of a colonised land. The Burghers, conscious of their European lineage, take on the British customs as matter of right. A similar display of authority is made by the Burghers in their appropriation of the customs, manners, language and practices of the native Ceylonese people. They simultaneously assume and reject their European and Ceylonese lineages. They put themselves in a superior position than both the British and the Ceylonese, from the British because of the native associations and a natural greater right over Ceylon, and from the natives because of the affinity with the English. It is crucial to note that Burghers' sense of selfhood depends largely on their otherness i.e., their distance from both the English and the Ceylonese.

As *Running in the Family* progresses there emerges a dialogue between the multiple layers of authors own self, and his family, community, the variegated patterns of history, memory and past, the fragile and obstinate ties with the Ceylonese culture and landscape. If there is a single statement that brings out the precarious nature of Ondaatje's relationship with the island, it has to be located in the section entitled 'Karapothas', the native Sri-Lankan word for the term 'foreigner': "I'm the foreigner, I'm the prodigal who hates the foreigner" (79). Ondaatje is a 'foreigner among foreigners in a foreign land' (Jewinski, 115), and is still the prodigal because the place is his home and was that of his ancestors for more than five centuries.

The position does not allow Ondaatje to adopt a singular perspective. Ondaatje returns back to his island home not simply as a prodigal or a foreigner as he is none of the two completely. He approaches the island as one of the imperialists as well, with expanded horizons Ondaatje attempts to take in the essence of all the possible threads of fascination that pulled the colonial powers towards the island and sustained those who lived in it. Ondaatje is at once the first Ondaatje to land on the island back in the year

1600; a prudent and affluent Ondaatje amassing vast fortune for himself through his deft tackling of the British colonial practices; a suave and eccentric Marvin Ondaatje getting involved in notorious drunken escapades and the writer Michael Ondaatje returning home after twenty-five years.

Ondaatje writes, "I had already planned the journey back. During quiet afternoons I spread maps onto the floor and searched out possible routes to Ceylon" (22). The act may appear a little made up, as it would have been a little more practical if Ondaatje simply inquired about the flights available to Sri Lanka. Perhaps he did, but a phone call to an airlines office could never have communicated the significance of the move for him and the magnitude of the perspective with which he looks towards the island. By spreading the maps and attempting to search possible routes to Ceylon, Ondaatje fictionalises, historicises and romanticises his move and brings into stark relief the complexity and the multiplicity of his perspective, as if it cannot be otherwise, as if every journey back home has to begin with maps, the concrete representations on paper.

Michael Ondaatje, peering at the maps of Ceylon, attempts to appropriate the gaze of his first ancestor and the other European imperial voyagers, invaders, adventure seekers eager to make a mark, in search of money and manhood spurned, enticed by the dreams of Asia. The concern with cartography is crucial to Ondaatje as it was for them. But what fascinates Ondaatje particularly is not the static nature of lines on the maps but their indeterminate nature, casual, liquid, like rumours caught up in transformations. The exactness of the island's shape and its contours has emerged through cartographic translations and Ondaatje finds himself irresistibly intrigued by imaginative mappings of the island that preceded its exactness:

The section 'Tabula Asiae' depicts the great rumours of topography, more imaginative than scientific:

> On my brother's wall in Toronto are the false maps. Old portraits of Ceylon. The result of sightings, glances from the trading vessels, the theories of sextant. The shapes differ so much they seem to be translations – by Ptolemy, Mercator, Francois,

Figure 1 ***Ptolemy, 200 A.D.***

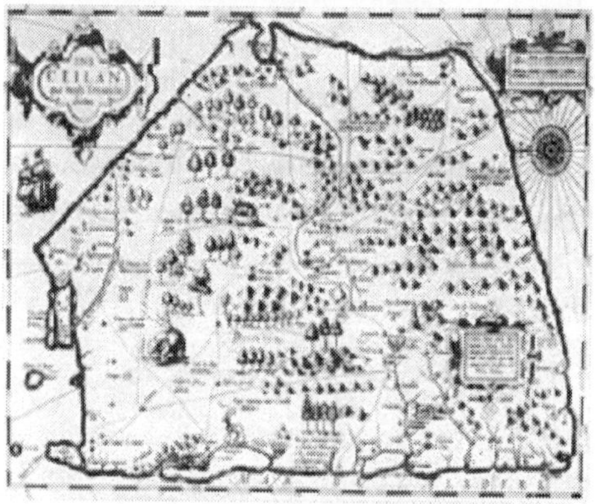

Figure 2 ***Mercator-Hondius, 1609***

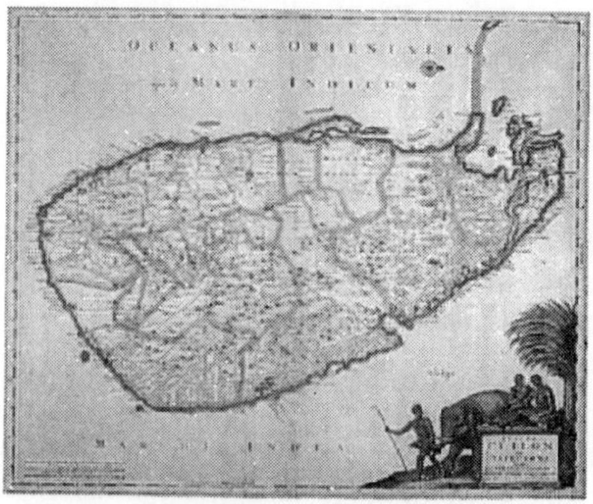

Figure 3 ***Nikolaas Visscher, 1680***

> Valentyn, Mortier, and Heydt – growing from mythic shapes into eventual accuracy. Amoeba, then stout rectangle, and then the island we know it now, a pendent off the ear of India. (63)

These *rumours of topography* (refer to Figures 1, 2, and 3) are significant as they hold the delicate threads that go into the making of the fabric of Ceylon not only in terms of cartography but also in terms of the historical and cultural evolving of the Ceylonese people. The relationships that were forged, sought, and eventually established or deserted while the island reached the accuracy of cartographic depiction; the country and culture evolved within the rumours of topography, the factual lost and unimportant within the plethora of translations. Ondaatje appears to equate inaccuracy with translations but here the order is reversed as the translations preceded the original and made its cartographic accuracy possible through their inaccuracies.

Indeterminacy, transformations gradual and sudden, the wet layers of history, the un-historical left within the margins of history, 'things moving to the clear', are crucial Ondaatjean concerns and they are reflected in his approach towards cartography, history (personal, official, unofficial or alternative histories); in his treatment of time and space and the finer nuances of individual identity. It is almost a desire to be in the green room, watching the actors' metamorphosis into characters they are about to play on stage or to be there seconds before a body transforms into a mummy. Ondaatje wants the precise lines of the Ceylonese map to melt, to whisper the rumours of topography that preceded them, he wants to be witness to all the christenings of the island, and the best man in all the marriages of this 'wife of many marriages', wants her to speak of the intimacy and pains which appear to vaporise with names, nationalities, and the dead chronology of official history.

Running in the Family, in all its picturesque, exotic descriptions and instances of high life of a lost generation, brings the blatant alienation of an entire community and its gradual dissipation into nothingness. Ondaatje is careful to take notice of the deliberate distance that his ancestors maintained from the natives whether it was their high life, big bungalows or the grand stands from which the natives in the 'Gandhi enclosures' appeared like *ants* (49). But Ondaatje's vision does not have the conceit of his ancestors. In the book, he attempts to understand the voices that his ancestors ignored and in his childhood he did not know they existed. Ondaatje quotes a poem from Lakdasa Wikkramasinha:

> Don't talk to me about Matisse ...
> The European style of 1900, the tradition of the studio
> where the nude woman reclines forever
> on a sheet of blood
> Talk to me of the culture generally –
> how the murderers were sustained
> by the beauty robbed of savages: to our remote
> villages the painters came, and our white-washed
> mud-huts were splattered with gunfire.
>
> (85–86)

Significantly enough, the voice finds a place in the section titled 'Karapothas', among the foreign voices of D.H. Lawrence, Leonard Woolf, Robert Knox and Edward Lear. Ondaatje juxtaposes contradictory claims, visions and perceptions so while Leonard Woolf says, "All jungles are evil"(78), a Ceylonese legend claims, "From Seyllan to Paradise is forty miles, the sound of the fountains of Paradise is heard here"(81). Ondaatje refers to the 5th century graffiti poems 'which spoke of love in all its confusions and brokenness' (84), and follows it up with a reference to the poems written on walls by the insurgents in 1971 the poems that spoke of the 'struggle, tortures, the unbroken spirit, love of friends who had died for the cause' (84). While the colonial powers splattered the mud-huts of the natives with gunfire, after independence their own government executed them and covered the poems with 'whitewash and lye'.

The juxtaposition of these contradictory voices underlies Ondaatje's characteristic relationship with the island. His distance makes him see the relativity and the relevance of each voice and version. He is neither a complete foreigner like Lawrence or Woolf nor a native like Lakdasa or the insurgent poets. And he is not 'lost' in the sense in which the people of his parents' generation were. He cannot disown any of the voices or claims as they are partially ingrained in him and yet he has to find his own version of the land.

In fact, Ondaatje finds his version of the land, discovers the way to relate to it. He relates to it in poetry. The generic choice is crucial as the eccentricity and raucous dancing of the Burgher generation of the 1920s and the 1930s to the melody of imported songs finds an expression in prose, and lime-burners, cinnamon peelers, and the women turning into the old pleasure of darkness into their homes, the 5th century portraits of beautiful women in Sigiri hills, the people and facets of the land that Ondaatje's ancestors ignored, become the subjects of his poems. Ondaatje captures a beautiful moment in the poem 'High Flowers':

> The woman my ancestors ignored
> sits at the doorway chopping coconut
> cleaning rice.
>
> Her husband moves
> in the air between trees
>
> (87)

Ondaatje's ancestors might have casually overlooked the woman but he finds himself in a position to relate to her. Ondaatje does not seek to belong to the island in the way in which his ancestors did or the old Burgher lady whom Ricardo Orizio quotes:

> We Burghers have become strangers in our own land. We have given so much, created so much. And now that I'm old, it sometimes happens at a reception that someone will ask me where I come from and how long have I lived in their beautiful country. They take me for a tourist, or missionary. I tell them that my ancestors have probably been here longer than theirs. But the old times are gone forever. My parents and their friends would go horse-racing, then on to diner, then dance until dawn. Then they would jump in their cars and dash down to the beach for a swim … .[3]

The old lady sounds like one of Ondaatje's aunts and her statement speaks of the trauma of the Burghers in general but her nostalgia for a glorious past of horse-racing, dinner and dance points at an inevitable alienation that might not have been felt in the days of affluence of the Burghers but was sure to narrow down upon them eventually. Ondaatje explores his past and lost family ties but not with the overtones of nostalgia of the old lady or the Burghers who live under the perennial shadows of 'the loss of paradise' nausea.

In the process of running in the family, Ondaatje discovers his way, his desire of belonging to the island. The poem "Cinnamon Peeler" asserts the Ondaatjean desire:

> If I were a cinnamon peeler
> I would ride your bed
> and leave the yellow bark dust
> on your pillow ...
> you could never walk through markets
> without the profession of my fingers
> floating all over you. The blind would
> stumble certain of whom they approached ...
> what good is it
> to be the lime burner's daughter
> left with no trace
> as if not spoken to in the act of love
> as if wounded without the pleasure of a scar.
>
> (95–96)

Ondaatje wants to be the Cinnamon Peeler, wants his certainty of belonging whereby the blind may know *whom they approached*. He desires the pride and the assurance of the Cinnamon Peeler's wife, does not want to be *wounded without the pleasure of a scar*, wants to be *spoken to in the act of love*. The depth of this desire provides a context to Ondaatje's otherness and puts him outside the otherness of his community. Ondaatje wants all the scars of his multicultural, multiethnic belongings to be visible, to be made translatable through history, memory, myth, legend, rumour or the *well told* lies that are considered *worth a thousand facts in Sri Lanka* (206).

Ondaatje knows that you have to own the land you live in or you are aliens or invaders. He is caught up in the desire to return and belong but is also aware that the more he runs in to his family the farther he gets away from it. His version of the land is going to remain personal it cannot be equated with that of the family left behind on the island. The Burghers are the progeny of the conscious colonial plot that let loose, and evolved beyond the authorial colonial desire and with the authors gone the plot slipped into numerous sub-plots, overlappings and lost meaning in the margins and those who could locate meaning and discover a pattern of belonging in all the chaos, paradoxically are the Jonahs, the prodigals who left the island and acquired the distance of time and space.

Ondaatje puts together 'another family'[4] in *In the Skin of a Lion*. This time the family is of the immigrants who came to Canada, his adopted home, in the first quarter of the twentieth century. The novel has received critical acclaim for voicing of the 'un-official' histories of the making of Toronto and in some ways of Canada. The novel does it to some extent but it cannot be reduced to the formulaic attempts of the peripheries against the center, left against right, the privileged against the unprivileged. In fact what it does is to disturb the seemingly established order of history, its making, the fixed frames of identity, and brings to the foreground suppressions and resistance. It brings off hinges the oppressive, linear, progressive impositions of the few in power in the making of the nation and the production of its history.

Ondaatje through his text renders everything, considered to be stable and fixed, vulnerable where a slight shift may alter everything. Moreover, he counters stasis captures characters, situations, the city and the text in transit as they move toward varied metamorphosis. While the novel dismantles the hierarchies and dislocates centres, it looks for belongingness, a gradual evolvement of community and companionship through shared histories and spaces in spite of and beyond the official will.

The structuring of the novel is heralded by the opening epigraphs. The first is from the Babylonian epic of Gilgamesh, which incidentally is also the source of the title of the novel:

> The joyful will stoop with sorrow, and when you have gone to the earth I will let my hair grow long for your sake, I will wander through wilderness in the skin of a lion.

The second is from John Berger:

> Never again will a single story be told as though it were the only one.

While the first epigraph underlines the mythical framework of the novel and speaks of a quest initiated with a sense of loss, the second comes both as a thematic and structural concern for Ondaatje. The quest does not turn out to be a single story, in fact what Ondaatje does is to weave together a number of stories and quests in a curious relationship with points of confluence, concurrence and departure where the stories run both independent and intersect each other in time and space.

It is crucial to acknowledge the time frame within which Ondaatje situates the novel. The novel focuses primarily on the first quarter of the twentieth century, and the period has a vital significance for a number of reasons. First, Europe during this period was experiencing crisis; in the year 1913, just a year before the First World War, almost 4,00,000 immigrants primarily from European countries came to Canada, the event coincided with the creation of new provinces in Canada and the westward expansion of the country.[5]

The immigration of European people had multiple effects on the nation's growth to maturity. While it allowed the country to expand into newer territories it also brought the necessary work force to boost up the industrial growth and the making of Canada. In the pre-war period Canada profited from the prosperous world economy and established itself as an industrial as well as an agricultural power. Immigration strengthened Canadian economy; it was also acceptable because of the European origins of the immigrants. In the post-Second World War period, the trends of immigration were to change and this time a large majority of the immigrants were to be from the other parts of the globe, southern Europeans, Asians, South Americans and people from the Caribbean islands.

Immigration had its advantages both in terms of Canadian economy and culture but at the same time it brought its own problems, which ironically had to do with the economy and the culture of the country. The immigrants settled primarily in the cities as they required jobs and the industries located in the cities fulfilled the requirement but somehow the meagre wages failed to provide them decent conditions of living. Even the environments of the production houses were not healthy and the nature of the work claimed the health and lives of the people. The Great Depression soon followed it in 1929 that left one out of every four workers jobless. The times of strain were to continue for ten years but with the beginning of the Second World War Canada emerged from the economic depression. The advent of the war created demands that the Canadian industry was able to meet. Ondaatje situates his work during this period of crisis that played a fundamental, formative role in Canadian history.

The primary concern of the novel is migration and metamorphosis, the challenges faced by immigrant communities as they struggle to find a footing in the adopted home, and the systematic elimination of their role in the building of the nation from the nation's history. Immigration is, whether forced or voluntary, a complex act. It involves multiple dislocations – of geo-political spaces, culture, sensibilities – and forces the hitherto unquestioning individual to discover and negotiate his or her own identity in terms of belonging.

Ondaatje's novel explores the immigrant experience in its challenges and manifold manifestations but the attempt is not to produce a homogeneous or universal authentic account of the immigrant experience but the novel reveals the harsh and the lighter shades as an immigrant crosses boundaries, enters a new landscape and attempts to come to terms with it.

Immigrants abound in the novel – there are Finnish loggers, Macedonian labourers, Greeks, Italians – together they form the working class of the country. In fact, Ondaatje broadens the limits of the act of immigration, it becomes an act not only of the dislocation of people between nations but also of dislocations that take place within a nation and are not merely geographical in nature but psychological and emotive. Everyone is a stranger in the city; they have come across physical and mental landscapes to be a part of it. They chart and map the city in their own ways, holding on to their versions, relating to it, claiming it in their own ways. It is not only the immigrants but also people born in Canada like Patrick, Commissioner Harris, Alice, Clara and Hazen Lewis, are strangers in the way they forge their identities and relate to the city in their characteristic manners.

There are stories of immigrants arriving in Toronto from different countries, stories of immigrants arriving into the metropolis from the unknown, unmarked regions within the country, alongside the grand official story of the building of Toronto. The immigrants arrive in the city escaping economic depravity or political persecution at home, fuelled by dreams of success and tall tales of the returning immigrants. Their journey to the land of possibilities has not been an easy one, it is only their singular determination and practically nothing to fall back upon back home which sees them through the tortures of taking trains, sleeping in godowns, huddling up in carriage ships, encountering hunger, sickness, death and even then there are only a fortunate few who make it to the shores of Upper America.

Nicholas Temelcoff is one such immigrant to the city, he too had been charmed by the childhood stories, the fairy tales of Upper America told by 'those who returned to the Macedonian villages, those first travellers who were the judas goats to the west' (44). The *Judas goat* for Nicholas and his villagers was Daniel Stoyanoff who came back to the village and bought a farm with the money he received as compensation for losing an arm in a meat factory accident. He did not mind the loss; in fact he displayed the stump as a badge of his intelligence forcing them to think that they all were fools. He told them that in Upper America everything was 'rich and dangerous' (44), a risk worth taking. It was this 'spell of language' (43) that brought Nicholas and many others to Canada.

Then there are others, activists like Cato who bring an inheritance of struggle against exploitation from their home countries into Canada, Caravaggio the Italian thief, Small the 'immigrant rat' who had to win all or lose all and Patrick who comes from within Canada's hinterland escaping the whiteness of his childhood's landscape towards the colours of the city, looking for a job and life. As they move into the metropolis they counter forces that operate outside and within them. The complex architectonics of the city's multiplicity forms a dialectical relationship with the self of the individuals who try to find a place in it.

From his very childhood Patrick is aware of the presence of the immigrants who came as loggers in the winters and disappeared like the moths; though they have been coming for years they are cautious in their approach:

> Sometimes, he knows, this collection of strangers will meet the cows being brought in from pasture barn for milking and there will be a hushed politeness as they stand to the side of the road holding up the lanterns (one step back and they will be in a knee-high snowdrift), to let the cows lazily pass them on the narrow road. Sometimes the men put their hands on the warm flanks of these animals and receive their heat as they pass. They put their thin-gloved hands on these black and white creatures, who are barely discernible in the last of the night's darkness. They must do this gently, without any sense of attack or right. They do not own this land as the owner of the cows does. (7)

The hushed politeness of this community of strangers, pushing themselves to the edge, maintaining a perilous balance between assertion and a desire of contact speaks of their keen awareness of the boundaries that somehow persist. Even though they help in building the town with there manual labour, some lose their lives due to hardships, they have little contact with the town and its inmates. Their presence is muted, declared not by a human language but by the strokes of their axes in the woods, or the silent procession of lanterns early in the morning. It takes years for Patrick to learn the origins of these strangers who were his silent companions in the winter mornings.

Patrick, however, has another group of equally mute seasonal companions, the moths that come in the summers and stick themselves to his kitchen window. The strangers and the moths come alternately, captivating Patrick's imagination and demanding knowledge, translatability of mutual fascination into words:

> Perhaps he can haunt these creatures. Perhaps they are not mute at all, it is just a lack of range in his hearing. (When he was nine his father discovered him lying on the ground, his ear against the hard shell of cow shit inside which he could hear several bugs flapping and knocking.) He knows the robust call from the small

> bodies of cicadas, but he wants conversation – the language of the damsel flies who need something to translate their breath the way he uses the ocarina to give himself a voice, something to leap with over the wall of this place. (10)

Patrick's fascination for the strangers speaks of a desire to know the other, to translate this silent relationship of presence in the same landscape and the seasonal appearance into one, which has a language. It also underlies his fascination for the exotic as he looks into his school geography book, the maps of the world, mouthing the exotic names Caspian, Nepal, Durango and feels the texture of the pebbled cover and the coloured dyes that create the map of Canada (9). But knowing the other requires a *leaping over the wall of the place.* Patrick's childhood imagination is captured by these alternative existences of the moths and the loggers in his landscape, while they produce a longing for contact in him they also make him aware of the visible and invisible boundaries that exist in and around him, the boundaries that have to be crossed somehow.

The awareness of boundaries and walls pervades in the novel, both the immigrants and the inhabitants sense them, each responding in different ways. Patrick, as he arrives in Toronto, encounters on the Union Station a man with three suitcases shouting out in another language, he returns two days later to find the man in the same place, 'still unable to move from his safe zone, in a different suit, as if one step away was the quicksand of the new world' (54). Nicholas, Commissioner Harris, Caravaggio, Cato, Clara, the bridge, tannery and tunnel workers are all aware of boundaries as they move between them and with them.

The knowledge of the boundaries is the knowledge of space and the self and the other. There are the boundaries of colonial inheritance (in both individual and national contexts), class, race, language, and perspectives; with them the individuals appear to be caught up in self-prisons. In the beginning, the novel produces an impression of a collection of loners – Hazen Lewis, Patrick, Nicholas, Carravaggio, Harris, Alice, Clara, Small – who have walls around them and even the groups of workers appear segregated. Hazen Lewis, taciturn and abashed, remains as invisible as possible, Patrick, his son, slides through company unnoticed, Nicholas hooks his sight to objects and remains aloof, Caravaggio operates in the solitary comfort of the night, Harris appears locked with his obsession of concretising his dream visions of the city into reality, Small with his secrets remains an enigma, Alice, 'reveals no past, remains sourceless like those statues of men with wrapped hands who symbolized undiscovered rivers' (74); and though Patrick loves the eroticism of Clara's past he keeps losing and getting the parts of her and Small loves her because of her 'unfinished nature' (93). But their co-existence, the brushes with the other, impositions and resistance challenge boundaries, exposes and makes them vulnerable and the barriers fragile.

Proximity of diverse cultures, whether willed, imposed or accidental, plays a crucial role, prepares the ground for transformation and metamorphosis. Individuals and identities cannot remain static as the shapes of the city around them. Commissioner Harris knows it; he quotes Baudelaire, "the form of a city changes faster than the heart of a mortal" (109). So too Alice and Patrick, as Alice quotes her favourite lines from Conrad, "I have taught you that the sky in all its zones is mortal … . Let me now re-emphasize the extreme looseness of all structures" (135). The transformations are both gradual and sudden. Patrick turns from a village boy to a searcher, from a searcher to a tannery worker, to a tunneller, to an activist threatening to destroy the water plant, and eventually into Hanna's adopted father; Hazen Lewis from a farmer to a dynamiter; Nicholas from a daredevil at the bridge to a baker; Alice from a nun to an actress and into an activist voicing the migrant cause; Ambrose Small from the jackal of the Toronto business world to a runaway hiding out with his love Clara.

There are moments of sudden realisation, flashes of insight that reveal hidden knowledges, the mysteries of the other pulling one towards metamorphosis. Alice, the nun, after her miraculous save by Nicholas, shocked, speechless sits with him in a Macedonian bar (a completely alien place for her) as Nicholas, in extreme pain, mumbles few endearments and sleeps. Those few moments transform Alice forever; she realises the strangeness of this place has a meaning. She is able to discover this meaning only because she falls out, though accidentally, from the bridge and symbolically from the hierarchy of the ecclesiastical order. She feels how the darkness, the colour of the furniture around her represented a Balkan night, 'Now the arbour-like wallpaper makes sense to her. Now the parrot has a language' (37). She stands up looks at her image in the mirror, 'A woman whose hair was showing, caught illicit' (38). But she turns away from the image, puts her face to the zinc counter that 'was an edge of another country. She puts her ear against the grey ocean of it. Its memory of the day's glasses. The spill and the wiping cloth. Confessional. Tabula Rasa' (39), cuts her black habit into a skirt, takes the parrot Alicia's name and walks out. Metamorphosed. Even Nicholas is transformed by the experience:

> When he walks into the fresh air outside the Ohrida Lake Restaurant, on the morning after the accident, he sees the landscape as something altered, no longer so familiar that it is invisible to him. Nicholas Temelcoff walks now seeing Parliament Street from the point of view of the woman .... (48)

It is not just the accident or the act of saving that transforms Alice and Nicholas 'but those moments since' (49). The moments of togetherness, a shocked woman, a man in pain, the meeting of two alien shores, without much conversation, become the defining moments of their lives.

Patrick has seen around himself so many transformations that his perception is haunted by it:

> In the midst of his love for Alice, in the midst of lovemaking even, he watches her face wanting for her to be translated into this war bride or that queen or shopgirl, half expecting metamorphosis as they kiss. Annunciation. The eye would go first, and as he draws back he will be in another country, another century, his arms around a stranger. (152–153)

Closely akin to the transformations that occur in the novel is the deliberate assumption of roles, taking on the skins and the colours of the other, the frequently changing subject positions and altered perspectives. The skin imagery has a vital significance. The changing of skins has multiple implications, they are imposed by the establishment, assumed by the individuals to camouflage their identity but more importantly they symbolise changing of subject positions, taking responsibility. Patrick's experience in the tannery teaches him important lessons about identity and the pain of the others. The tannery workers leap into pools cut into stone, filled with colours, embracing the skins of recently slaughtered animals and in the process, 'the men stepped out in colours up to their necks, pulling wet hides out after them so it appeared they had removed the skin from their own bodies. They had leapt into different colours as if into different countries' (130). And when these men, after the work, stand under hot showers, the adopted skins fall to their feet, bringing them back to their own colours but the smell never leaves them. These men do not step into different skins and colours willingly but they are made to by the Canadian labour industry and though they might appear 'aesthetically plumaged' (130), in a winter morning to an unsuspecting eye, it is only they who are aware of the horrors of the 'aesthetics' of working in a tannery. As with the skins they assume during the work they have been given another skin by the establishment, the labour agent gives them English names, they assume these false identities and, 'remembered the foreign syllables like a number' (132), so they know each other by their 'false names or true countries' (135).

Colours and skins are also used as disguises. Carravaggio, the thief, colours himself blue in the colour of the prison roof (which again was a creation of an illusion of sky, humiliation of the senses) he was supposed to paint with Patrick and by doing so he wins his freedom. He holds fast to the dictum, 'Demarcation that is all we need to remember' (179). Remembering demarcation, the dividing lines, not so much to confine oneself but to obliterate difference to slide through differences. Later in the novel Carravaggio assumes the funny name Randolph Frog and by assuming the manners of the rich slides through their company with remarkable ease (222). Patrick too camouflages himself twice in the novel by putting grease on his body, for ironically similar purposes, earlier in his town Bellrock to dislodge the logs stuck in the river by putting dynamite under them (17) and later to bring off hinges the oppressive establishment by swimming through the lake, disguised in the blackness of grease to dynamite the water purification plant (227).

However, the strongest use of the changing of skins in the novel is that of a willing assumption of roles and responsibilities. Spearey remarks, "The skins that each character wears can be seen as manifestations of various personalities and subject positions rather than disguises which serve to conceal an essential and predetermined character" (Spearey, 52). Though, as shown already, the skins have been used as disguises and impositions in the novel but Spearey refers to the most potent manifestation of the wearing of skins in the novel. The flight from one true self to another, the changing of skins is, in a powerful way, a manifestation of shared responsibility, speaks of an intimacy for the other, a *leaping over the walls*, the terrible barriers of the self. Alice tells Patrick about a play in which several actresses shared the role of the heroine. After a while the powerful matriarch removes her large coat, 'from which animal pelts dangled and she passed it, along with her strength, to one of the minor characters. In this way even a silent daughter could put on the cloak and be able to break through her chrysalis into language. Each person had their moments when they assumed the skins of wild animals, when they took responsibility for the story' (157).

The passing on of skins and sharing of roles by different individuals is also manifested in the way in which Ondaatje treats the basic myth of Gilgamesh that runs through the structure of the novel in complex ways. Ondaatje substantially transforms the myth that is a classical example of the struggle between domineering centre (Gilgamesh) and the resisting periphery (Enkidu). Ondaatje dislocates the hierarchy of the myth, so at one point Harris with the impositions of his plans over the city is Gilgamesh, at another Patrick getting into the water plant is Gilgamesh. At the same time Patrick is Enkidu challenging the authority of Gilgamesh (Harris). Nicholas the daredevil, Cato the activist and the others who build the city with their labour are also Enkidus in different capacities. The temple woman who civilises Enkidu in the epic appears as Alice, the nun, in the novel but she plays an extended role like Patrick as she not only transforms Patrick but herself takes on the responsibility of challenging the establishment's oppressions. And it is her death that makes Patrick (like Gilgamesh) come down 'like an arrow' (242), straight into Harris' water plant.

Thus, the changing of skins involves not only changing subject positions but at the same time it demands participation, a sharing of responsibilities an intimate engagement with the other. Taking the skin on is a mutual transference of qualities. The skin and its wearer transform each other in complex ways. Alice's performance at the water-works captures Patrick into transformation, Alice dressed as a puppet is surrounded by real puppets that represent authority, there is the gap of language, the live puppet is incriminated, burdened with charges and it wants to cry out, to express its pain but the language and the words remain elusive. It starts banging its hand on the floor, the hand goes manic, demanding and at this moment Patrick intervenes, goes on to the stage to stop that hand, he does that only to learn later that every time this act was performed, someone from the audience intervened (118). The act compels Patrick to come out of himself, to share the pain, to take responsibility.

Chrysalis, the inability to express, works as a barrier and brings in the significance of acquisition of language, a voice and the need to make the expression a vehicle not only of sharing and companionship but also of claiming acknowledgement, acceptance and empowerment in socio-cultural, political and economic terms. The immigrants to the city attempt to learn the new language, it works both as a necessity, and desire to be accepted in the new home and is also imposed by the system. Ondaatje records the interesting ways in which the immigrants learn English, movies and theatre play a vital role in the linguistic appropriation of the adopted home. The immigrants learned their English from the recorded songs or through mimicking actors on stage so that by the end of the production of a play at the Fox or the Parrot theatres, 'the actors' speeches would be followed by growing echoes as Macedonians, Finns, and Greeks repeated the phrases after a half-second pause, trying to get the pronunciation right' (47), and they master it to such perfection that when one of the famous actors died during a performance, a Sicilian butcher took over, 'knowing his lines and his blocking meticulously' (47). And this way the immigrants, the outsiders of another language, 'walked out of their accent into regional American voices' (47). Nicholas learns English obsessively because he knows without the language he will be lost and as he sleeps he has translation dreams, 'in dreams the trees changed not just their names but their looks and character. Men started answering in falsettos. Dogs spoke out fast to him as they passed him on the streets' (46–47).

Learning the language, appropriating the accent of the other is not a simple switch over to another language but it transforms imagination, sensibility, the habit of the mind and character. But there are other barriers that have to be negotiated by the immigrant even as he learns the new language *meticulously.* As with the knowledge of boundaries and the desire to cross them, comes the desire to claim space and here the immigrant finds himself in difficult waters. As there are empirical, official, political and capitalistic wills at work and their corresponding imposition of form and charting of the cityscape, there are resistances that develop from the peripheries that the singularly progressive vision of those with power fails to take into consideration. Commissioner Harris the Head of Public Works, is relentless in the concretisation of his visions for the city. The Bloor Street Viaduct and the grand water plant are his version of the city. But with all his perseverance to see the projects through he fails to see, to acknowledge the death, pain and loss of those who transform his dreams into reality. When asked about the number of deaths of the workers during the building of the bridge Harris claims ignorance (236), the establishment, the newspaper headlines and the christening of the bridge, "Prince Edward" (27), betray nothing about its real makers.

Harris might claim ignorance of the horrors of working through nights on the bridge, of being lowered with animals into the depth of the earth tunneling till the bones rattled, carrying the smell of dead animals from the tanneries to the bed but he is equally ignorant or does not want to acknowledge the acts of resistance, played out right in the spaces he has charted, *his* spaces. The groups of immigrants, the workers of different nationalities with their wives and children trespass into the water plant that Harris adores and obsessively guards, for their weekly meetings (115). Earlier in the novel, the night before the public inauguration of the Bridge, the workers claim it before anyone else could, they 'moved with their own flickering lights – their candles for the bridge dead – like a wave of civilization, a net of summer insects over the valley' (27). And even the next day, before any show car containing officials may claim the bridge, a cyclist emerged from somewhere and dodged the officials to claim the bridge in its virginity and he was greeted with applause at the other end (27). These are little but vital gestures of resistance to impositions and erasures and they point alternative existences at different levels within the same space of the city, existences that do not require official authentication, and heroes like Nicholas who never make it to the front pages, 'Even in archive photographs it is difficult to find him' (34), but are to be sought with care, indicated only by a blur of intent in the photo graphs.

Patrick, uninitiated, too does not know anything about the union struggles up North and the murder of Cato, 'And all his life Patrick had been oblivious to it, a searcher gazing into the darkness of his own country, a blind man dressing the heroine' (157). He learns about this face of his country, where he has lived all his life, only when he finds himself in the middle of the 'irony of reversals' (133), when he comes to live with the community of the strangers from his childhood, a stranger among strangers.

Harris, Patrick, Small, Nicholas, Carravaggio, Alice everyone attempts to control and chart space in their own manners. Harris by his structures, Patrick by his desire to command the spaces of the others, Small by his predatory hovering over the Toronto business world, Nicholas by his free falling under the bridge converting blank space into time Caravaggio by his acute awareness of landscape around him, and Alice with her cause and theatre performances. And then there are larger spaces; the localities, shops and restaurants that are the replicas of the home countries. But even in the midst of all these spaces and the desires to control them, the very fact of simultaneous existences and corresponding wills at work bring about a conflict that blocks singular determinations of space from any perspective whether imposed by the establishment or evolved by the resisting peripheries. A conflict that has to be negotiated by a reaching out, and a reordering.

Patrick learns an important lesson about space in a little accident with Clara, the lesson holds the key to Ondaatje's approach in the book:

> He positions Clara on the bed and tells her not to move. Then he takes off into the room – at first using his hands for security then ignoring them, just throwing his body within an inch of the window swooping his head down parallel to shelves while he rushes across the room in straight lines, in curves, as if he has the

mechanism of a bat in his human blood. He leaps across the bed delighted at her shriek. He is magnificent. He is perfect, she thinks. (80)

The initial fascination of Clara turns into restlessness and claustrophobia as she finds herself imprisoned by Patrick's movements, unable to move herself. She lowers herself from the bed and Patrick collides with her not anticipating her move. Spearey observes, 'In not allowing for any movement save his own, Patrick learns an "abrupt lesson" about the control of space' (Spearey, 54). So too Harris and others make a mistake as they fail to take into account the presence, the movements of others who inhibit the same space.

It is only through the realisation of the complexity of space, by inhibiting the skins of the others that Patrick is able to find order in his life and the chaotic surroundings. This is how Patrick learns about *the extreme looseness* of all structures and individual boundaries. Being transformed by Alice, in the water works performance; grieved by her death, Patrick assumes the role of her dead husband Cato and their cause and penetrates into the impenetrable water filtration plants, he puts dynamite all over the place and forces Harris to see the other side of his dreams in their horror, the face of the city that remains invisible to him.

The transformation that Patrick goes through is made possible only through his association with the landscapes of the others. Patrick constantly feels the need to align himself to others, 'He was always comfortable in someone else's landscape, enjoyed being taught the customs of a place. Patrick wants the city Hana had constructed for herself – the places she brought together and held as if on the delicate thread of curiosity' (138). Patrick was never taught any mythology by his father, there were only abrupt lessons to be learnt and remembered, he escapes from the whiteness of his childhood landscape remembering only to love things having to do with colours into the warmth and the colours of the city into the company of the strangers. He attaches himself obsessively with Clara, Alice, Nicholas, Small, Harris, Hana. Without these associations Patrick feels an emptiness, "Something hollow, so when alone, when not aligned with another ... he could hear the rattle within that suggested a space between him and community. A gap of love" (157). Patrick becomes a *prism* that brought together and refracted their various stories:

> His own life was no longer a single story but part of a mural, which was a falling together of accomplices. Patrick saw a wondrous night web – all of these fragments of a human order, something ungoverned by the family he was born into or the headlines of the day. A nun on a bridge, a daredevil who was unable to sleep without a drink, a boy watching a fire from his bed at night, an actress who ran away with a millionaire – the detritus of the age was realigned. (145)

In the tanneries the workers address each other by their nationalities, 'Hey Italy! And for Patrick the expression is 'Hey Canada!' (135). Ajay Heble, in "Putting Together Another Family: *In the Skin of a Lion*, Affiliation, and the Writing of Canadian (Hi)stories", notices, 'if Patrick is, even if for a few moments, Canada, the workers around him are also Canada not just a part of it' (Heble, 243). The workers of other nationalities address him by the name Canada because Patrick was born in Canada and there is the gap of language between them but in the process of the novel Patrick does manage to *be* the country, its extended metaphor, not because of his birth or language but by the way he aligns himself to others, feels an emptiness without them. Canada is the *mural*, the prism that brings together and refracts the lives of all those who live in it, has as many faces as those who move in it. Ondaatje counters the emptiness of singular cultural reflection (official or otherwise) with refraction that comes closer in defining cross-cultural or multicultural experiences by its openness, possibilities, embracing multiple reflections and counter-reflections in a dialectical, evolving relationship.

Ajay Heble, in his analysis of the novel, brings into consideration Edward Said's concept of "filiation" and "affiliation". In Said's formulation filiation refers to a seeking of relationships, primarily in the Second World (invader-settler colonies), of "direct genealogical descent" from the parent countries, England and France in the Canadian context. Affiliation on the contrary refers to the relationships that develop as a result of "social and political conviction, economic and historical circumstances, voluntary effort and willed deliberation." Said discovers the failure of the filiative ties in the Second World countries and refers to "the transition from a failed idea or possibility of filiation to a kind of compensatory order that, whether it is a party, an institution, a culture, a set of beliefs, or even a world-vision, provides men and women with a new form of relationship" (qtd. by Heble, 242). Heble traces how *In the Skin of a Lion* can be read in terms of Said's concept of affiliation, whereby there is the discovery of a new form of relationship between the immigrants and the country, a relationship that comes closer in defining Canadian identity than the filiative modes sought, maintained and advanced by the Canadian establishment.

Affiliation, the gradual evolvement of a compensatory order, is crucial not only in terms of defining national identity, but at the same time it has a vital significance for an expatriate as he tries to relate himself with both the spaces of his origin and of adoption. Ondaatje's *Running in the Family* explores filial ties and *In the Skin of a Lion* seeks affiliation with the adopted home, the former has a strong personal perspective and the later is more communal in nature. However, a juxtaposition of the two books reveals that even an attempt to claim the filial ties, family relations, histories, whether from an individual or national perspective, is possible only through a process of affiliation, an inclusion and negotiation of different relationships and threads of belonging towards the evolvement of a new relationship, a realigning of the entanglements of the self, other, and homes. Contrary to the desires, at individual, communal or national level to revert back to a past or to maintain nostalgic ties with it, this new compensatory order emerges from lived experiences, sharing and taking responsibilities, an order that arises out of and is manifested in the dynamics of geo-political, socio-cultural spaces not in the emptiness of abstract time.

With *Running in the Family* and *In the Skin of a Lion* Ondaatje contextualises the multiple layers of his being and belonging and those of others who are dislocated and undergo cross-cultural experiences. Both the books are not as much about the trauma of dislocation as they are about relocating and relocations. Between the spaces of these two books Ondaatje makes the alien shores of Sri Lanka and Canada and his belonging to them, meet as he explores the precarious boundaries between the self and the other, opens the room for negotiation and by deliberately inhibiting the skins of the others takes the responsibility to resist hierarchies, oppressive histories, seeking a human order, a realignment of identities and spaces, by exploding, like Patrick, the barriers, deadlocks, stasis. To sum up, Ondaatje does what Conrad demands of art (one of the voice sewn in *In the Skin of a Lion*):

> Only the best art can order the chaotic tumble of events. Only the best can realign chaos to suggest both the chaos and order it will become. (146)

Notes

1. Chamberlin's remark has been quoted from Susan Spearey's article, "Mapping and Masking: The Migrant Experience in Michael Ondaatje's *In the Skin of a Lion*." *Journal of Commonwealth Literature* (1995): 48.
2. By the year 1800 the Burghers were a community with mixed Portuguese, Dutch, Sinahalese and Tamil origins. Other European nationalities, with the passage of time, kept pouring in and the settlers, though there were not many, got absorbed in the Burghers. When the British conquered Ceylon in 1796, there were 900 Burgher families in Ceylon centred chiefly in Colombo, Galle, Matara and Jaffna. The references to the history of Burghers in Ceylon are from Marco Ramerini, "History of the Dutch in Ceylon (Sri Lanka): The Burgher of Ceylon", www.lankalibrary.com
3. The quotation from Ricardo Orizio has been taken from Jonathan, Yardley. "*Lost White Tribes* by Ricardo Orizio", www.wehaitians.com, Sunday, July 22, 2001; Page BW02.
4. The expression appears on the page 45 of the novel *In the Skin of a Lion* and has been used by Ajay Heble in the title of his paper, "Putting Together Another Family: *In the Skin of a Lion*, Affiliation, and the Writing of Canadian (Hi)stories." *Essays on Canadian Writing* 56 (1995).
5. The references to immigration in Canada are from the booklet *Facts on Canada* published by Canada Information Office, Website: www.infocan.gc.ca
6. The reference is from Ajay Heble's essay "Putting Together Another Family: *In the Skin of a Lion*, Affiliation, and the Writing of Canadian (Hi)stories", *Essays on Canadian Writing* 56, 236–54 (Fall, 1995).

Works Cited

Heble, Ajay. "Putting Together Another Family: *In the Skin of a Lion*, Affiliation, and the Writing of Canadian (Hi)stories". *Essays on Canadian Writing* 56, 236–54 Fall, 1995.

Jewinski, Ed. *Express Yourself Beautifully*. Toronto: ECW Press, 1994.

Ondaatje, Michael. *In the Skin of a Lion*. Toronto: McClelland and Stewart, 1987.

——. *Running in the Family*. Toronto: McClelland, 1982.

——. *Coming Through Slaughter* (1976). Picador, 1984.

——. *Collected Works of Billy the Kid: Left Handed Poems* 1970, Picador, 1989.

Ramerini, Marco. "History of the Dutch in Ceylon (Sri Lanka): The Burgher of Ceylon", www.lankalibrary.com

Spearey, Susan. "Mapping and Masking: The Migrant Experience in Michael Ondaatje's *In the Skin of a Lion*". *Journal of Commonwealth Literature*. No. 2, 45–60, 1995.

Yardley, Jonathan. "*Lost White Tribes* by Ricardo Orizio", www.wehaitians.com, Sunday, July 22, 2001; Page BW02.

4

'Imploding Time and Geography'*

Time, Space and Narrative

> Did it start with Bergson or before? Space was treated as the dead, the fixed, the undialectical, the immobile. Time, on the contrary, was richness, fecundity, life, dialectic. (Foucault, 22)

Time and space have a crucial significance in our experience of the world. They are central to both the experiential and the representational realms of human existence. Human life at any given moment is the product of the complex interplay of time and space. However, there is often a tilting of balance, as Foucault points out in the above statement, in favour of history and its linear accumulation of past. History presents itself as a homogeneous body not only recording events and happenings but forging connections in terms of cause and effect relationships and with the backing of these interdependent occurrings, history also usurps the claim to future happenings and shaping of the human world.

Edward W. Soja in *Postmodern Geographies* (1997) presents an incisive exploration of the silencing of space in critical social theory and the dissociation of time and space in the increasingly historical, progressive theories of the past and the contemporary

* Phrase used by Michael Ondaatje in *The English Patient* and subsequently by Rufus Cook as part of title of his article "Imploding Time and Geography: Narrative Compressions in Michael Ondaatje's *The English Patient*". *Journal of Commonwealth Literature*. No. 2. (1996), pp. 109–125.

discourses. Soja traces the history of the silencing of geography and the excessive veneration of history in his book. The radical questioning of the tyranny of history began in the 1980s but even before that, voices like those of Foucault and John Berger posited a challenge to the authority of history, bringing to the fore the vital significance of space. However Foucault's spatial turn was not pronounced as he apparently buried it in his 'brilliant whirls of historical insight' (Soja, 16). The most explicit of his pronouncements regarding space were expressed in a 1967 lecture 'Des Espaces Autres' but it received critical acknowledgement almost after twenty years when it was published in the French journal *Architecture-Mouvement-Continuite* (1984) and in the English translation by Jay Miskowiec in *Diacritics* (1986) as 'Of Other Spaces'. In the lecture Foucault spoke of the great obsession of nineteenth century with history and its themes of 'ever accumulating past' leading to 'a menacing glaciation of the world' and predicted a radical shift in attitude towards the dynamics of time and space in the twentieth century:

> The present epoch will perhaps be above all the epoch of space. We are in the epoch of simultaneity: we are in the epoch of juxtaposition, the epoch of the near and far, of the side-by-side, of the dispersed. We are at a moment I believe, when our experience of the world is less that of a long life developing through time than that of a network that connects points and intersects with its own skein. (Foucault, 22)

However, there were not many who shared Foucault's conviction. The idea of 'making history' remained obsessively invigorating to people whom Foucault calls 'the pious descendents of time' and it was perhaps too traumatic a thought to suddenly dislodge the blinkers that tied them to the linearity and sequentiality of time. Nevertheless Foucault's pronouncements did cause a stir even if a bit too late. Foucault's criticism does not entail a rejection of history, he kept his professed association with history all along his life, but is rather against 'historicism' and its tendency to ignore the vital significance of space in its historical master narrative, the tenacity with which it maintains its upward vertical march refusing to take into account the horizontal spatial perspective. Foucault's observations propose a radical challenge to the paradigmatic 'historicism' in the sociological imagination of critics like C. Wright

Mills. Mills' entrenched sociological imagination finds an emphatic expression in his statement:

> We have come to know that every individual lives, from one generation to the next, in some society: that he lives out a biography, and that he lives it out within some historical sequence. By the fact of his living he contributes, however minutely, to the shaping of this society and to the course of history, even as he is made by society and by its historical push and shove … . The sociological imagination enables us to grasp history and biography and the relations of the two within society … . No social study that does not come back to the problems of biography, of history, and of their intersections within society, has completed its intellectual journey. (qtd. by Soja, 13)

Soja discusses how Mills' statement reduces 'meaning and action to the temporal constitution and experience of social being' and denies geography any role whatsoever in the production of the social being. And though, as Soja points out, the historical imagination is never completely spaceless, the unconsciously written geographies of the critical social historians always have 'time' and 'history' as the primary variables thus in their works an 'already-made geography sets the stage, while the willful making of history dictates the action and defines the story line' (Soja, 14). Historicism tends to take space for granted, a backdrop in the making of history that does not have a role to play in its matrix of history, biography and social being. It is in this context that time signifies *richness, fecundity, life* and space remain on the periphery. The extreme position of historicism fails to take into account simultaneity, anything that may occur on the sidelines of the grand historical master narrative. Foucault could foresee the impossibility of the maintenance of the homogeneity of historicism in the context of the multiple juxtapositions of the opposites in the contemporary world.

Foucault, Berger, Soja and other postmodern geographers do not propose a denial of time or history but they seek to establish a dialectical relationship between the two as they influence our individual and collective lives on this planet. As Soja points out, it is "a call for an appropriate interpretive balance between space, time, and social being, or what may now more explicitly be termed the creation of human geographies, the making of history, and the constitution of society"(23). However, *an appropriate interpretive balance between space, time and social being* demands a radical reformulation of established narrative structures whether historical or otherwise. John Berger explicitly states the nature of the challenge in the context of the modern novel:

> We hear a lot about the crisis of the modern novel. What this involves, fundamentally, is a change in the mode of narration. It is scarcely any longer possible to tell a story sequentially unfolding in time. And this is because we are too aware of what is continually traversing the storyline laterally. That is to say, instead of being aware of a point as an infinitely small part of a straight line, we are aware of it as an infinitely small part of an infinite number of lines, as the centre of a star of lines. Such awareness is the result of our constantly having to take into account the simultaneity and extension of events and possibilities. (qtd. by Soja, 22)

The complex architectonics of time and space, interplay of cultures, histories, memories and myth, transformations, the formation and formulations of identity acquire a crucial significance in expatriate writing. There is a consistent engagement with the dynamics of time and space as the expatriate writers find themselves in a continual process of negotiation with the conflicting claims of disparate cultures, the immediacy of the geo-political and socio-cultural context of the adopted homes and the ingrained inheritance of diverse backgrounds of their countries of origin. Critics have seen the treatment of time and space by the expatriate writers with great interest as they engage themselves with writing about the inherited and adopted spaces or deliberately create 'third spaces' attempting to come to terms with the complexity of identity and its nuances through the subtle and violent transformations it undergoes by moving out of the implicatory position of specific spaces of inheritance and of adoption.

The choice of specific spaces has specific implications in terms of socio-political and cultural positioning of the expatriate. The choices of first, second or a deliberate creation of third spaces are complex moves. The expatriate writers in their treatment of adopted and inherited spaces primarily concentrate on issues that deal with their coming to terms with the new culture, the trauma of dislocation and a search for identity and roots in their past. As an expatriate steps out of both the countries of origin and of adoption into a third or a neutral space the dynamics of time, space and identity are opened up. The creation of a third space raises several fundamental questions vis-à-vis the first two spaces. Whether the creation of a third space entails a rejection of the detrimental specifics of the spaces of adoption and of origin, does the move involve an escape into a utopian realm of wish fulfilment or is it a deeper negotiation of the specifics through their dislocation from the spheres of influence, does the writer project a state of perennial homelessness or is it an attempt to feel at home in all the spaces through a seeking of connections in terms of histories, cultures or identities.[1]

Ondaatje, over the span of his literary career, has been engaged in exploring a diverse range of subjects and locales that reflect his characteristic concern with cross-cultural initiations and their impact on the formation of individual identity and modes of perception. An overview of his works reveals certain crucial shifts in his writings both at the thematic and structural levels. There has been a subtle transition in his choice of genres, he has shifted from poetry to a postmodernist mixing of genres writing fictional biographies (*The Collected Works of Billy the Kid* and *Coming Through Slaughter*), a memoir (*Running in the Family*) into the surer realms of novel writing, from individual subjects to collective situations, from the recreation of past eras of late nineteenth century and early twentieth century to the more recent era of 1980s in *Anil's Ghost* and from an apparently a – political stance of the earlier works to one that has visible political implications.

Location of a work in a specific space has important implications but even more important is the treatment of that space, the meeting of the narrative challenge that demands both time and space to have a dialectical relationship privileging none over the other. Ondaatje's locates *The English Patient* in a third space away from both Sri Lanka and Canada and in terms of time he chooses the last phase of the Second World War, a deliberate move from the contemporary to the historical. While the move has its significance from the expatriate perspective in relation to the questions of identity and belonging but at the same time the choice of Italy and the era of the world war has important artistic and intellectual implications. The juxtaposition of Italy that has a visible presence of high art with war has more in offering than any possible questions of identity and belonging may suggest. Italy with its long maintained and considerably preserved artistic tradition within the clutches of the war is Ondaatje's creation of a complex dynamics and aesthetics that goes beyond the claims of history or biography. Italy may appear a neutral space insofar as Ondaatje's countries of origin and of adoption dominate the critical perspective. But Italy's artistic tradition and the phenomena of war cannot be bound within a time or geography, as they virtually encompass the entire world, civilisation and its histories in its complex contradictory aspects of creation and destruction, the perennial conflict between artistic and political aspirations and the struggle for survival and sustenance. Ondaatje's projection of a time and a space too precariously balanced on the edge of order and chaos in *The English Patient* has profound implications as it explores and opens other times and spaces, histories and geographies in an interrelated, interdependent, mutually influencing set of relationships.

In Ondaatje's texts both time and space have multiple implications. Time brings in the immediate time-frame of the novel, the constant presence of history in a physical form and its master narrative, the counter and supplementary narratives of myth, legend and rumour, memory and as the novel unfolds these temporal devices converge and depart in significant ways. Space in Ondaatje is the immediate landscape projected in the novel, inner spaces embedded and evolving in the psyche of the characters, architecture and archaeology, individual, communal and nationalistic forging of geographical, social, cultural and political spaces, the physical space of the body and the awareness and projection of the novel and its text itself as a space and a construct. The different time frames and spaces simultaneously coexist and intersect with each other in Ondaatje's narrative. Ondaatje spatialises history and historicises space, each reflecting the other in their wondrous web of reflections and misreflections, the moments and junctures of confluence, concurrence and departures.

The immediate time frame in *The English Patient* is the last few months of the Second World War, the place is Italy and most of the action takes place in a villa. The novel operates within the historical context of the war and its sudden end with the dropping of the atom bombs over Hiroshima and Nagasaki. Ondaatje abides by the dates and very significantly the novel opens with an extract from the minutes of the Geographical Society meeting, 1940 London. The extract is a dedication to the death of Geoffrey Clifton and the disappearance of his wife Katharine Clifton 'during the 1939 desert expedition in search of Zerzura'. The novel has ten sections – The Villa, In Near Ruins, Some Time a Fire, South Cairo 1930–1938, Katharine, A Buried Plane, In Situ, The Holy Forest, The Cave of Swimmers and August. The sections do not reveal any linear order; reading out the names produces an impression of a loose grouping, an ensemble of spaces (The Villa, In Near Ruins, The Holy Forest, The Cave of Swimmers), time (Some Time a Fire, South Cairo 1930–1938, August), character (Katharine) and the two sections A Buried Plane and In Situ refer to positions. Within the apparently casual, loosely connected segments of the novel there are four major narrative strands corresponding to the four characters. Each character has his or her story as they arrive into the villa and stay in for different reasons. The coming together of these unrelated characters and their being in the villa is governed by time, a coincidence made possible by the larger deliberate action of war fought by nations impatient of their boundaries.

The English patient, Hana, Caravaggio and Kip have come from Hungary, Canada and India and are drawn into the war for entirely different reasons and though destroyed and maimed by the war, they are the survivors. Ondaatje's narrative moves back and forth both in time and space as it traces the tracks of each character walking into the villa and stepping out of it into the specific spaces of belonging. The villa is occupied as if only in transit and indicates an enclosed space. Yet what happens here, the relationships they develop, the memories they excavate both in others and themselves are embedded in their consciousness even as they move into future and are separated by geographical spaces.

Hana, Caravaggio and Kip have their pasts, that keep surfacing at different moments in the novel. However, there is a major difference in their stories of the past and that of the English patient, none of them is too keen to reveal his/her past unless faced with a specific question and even then there is a tendency to be evasive. Caravaggio keeps reminding Hana of the incidents from her childhood, to pull her out from her obsession with the English patient, but himself remains mute about his past. Kip with his self-sufficiency and concentration on the job moves around with the architecture of his past unrevealed, staying on the periphery. The stories and the past of Hana, Kip and Caravaggio, for a major part, find an expression in the authorial voice though within the voice of the author there are subtle shifts from third person to first person narrative, as if the character suddenly gets alive to his story, takes the responsibility for it or at other moments leaves it casually in the hands of the author.

The case of the English patient is different. The patient has the largest share of the narrative and when he speaks he opens up doorways between histories, memories, myths, legends, rumours, geographical expeditions, intricacies of music, art and literature, lost civilisations, shifting from one level to the other like a hawk, obliterating boundaries as the author allows him shift from the first person to the third person, slip from one age to another from one space to others. The patient peels off the layers of his consciousness and thoughts but remains discreetly evasive of his identity, as if he takes his burnt, expressionless face literally, no more interested in the identifications of names and nationalities. Within the novel he has been variously referred to as King David, Dadulas, and Odysseus and critics have traced the elements of Grail romance in the novel. But from the narrative standpoint, the English patient comes closer to the mythical figure of Tiresias, the man with shrunken breasts, who represents both the genders and is in a way above both in their limitations, the patient too is burnt beyond recognition and his sex neutralised by the accident, he sees connections and continuations that others do not and is able to bring together the threads of chaos, ascribing and reinscribing lost meanings and relationships.

The narrative of the war in the backdrop and the stories of the individual characters constitute a considerable part of the narrative but none of these narratives unfold in any sequential manner. The narrative progressions/digressions in the novel are determined by the opening of time and space in relation with the present moment and the space in the text. A momentary thought, a small incident, an aspect of the surrounding geography takes the narrative into different directions as it alternates between the past, the present and at times future projections.

The central aspect of Ondaatje's treatment of the dialectics of time and space is that time and history are opened up within the dynamics of space. Ondaatje delves deep into the vast stretches of deserts and landscapes, and the smaller spaces of buildings, books, bodies, music, paintings and statues. As he moves into these spaces he brings into consideration geography, cartography, archaeology and these spatial explorations depict a keen historical consciousness extending itself into the mythical. A close consideration of different spaces in Ondaatje reveals intricate patterns of relationships between these spaces and their histories.

The Villa San Girolamo has a crucial significance in this context. The villa has its own history. It is an old nunnery that was built to protect its 'inhabitants from the flesh of the devil' (43); it was taken over by the German army during the war as it had 'castlelike battlements', and with the retreat of the Germans, the Allies converted it into a temporary hospital. But the place had its dangers as there were hidden bombs everywhere in the villa and was eventually evacuated save for the patient and the nurse who simply refused to leave. However, as the novel progresses other possibilities regarding the past of the villa, its layers of history are opened up:

> I think this was the Villa Bruscoli. Poliziano – the great protégé of Lorenzo. I'm talking about 1483. In Florence, in Santa Trinita Church, you can see the paintings of the Medicis with Poliziano in the foreground, wearing a red cloak.
>
> ... Yes, I think a lot happened here. This fountain in the wall. Pico and Lorenzo and Poliziano and the young Michelangelo. They held in each hand the new world and the old world ... They sat in this room with a bust of Plato and argued all night. (56–57)

The villa, in all probability, could be the Villa Bruscoli that the patient claims it to be. The transformations that the villa has undergone in terms of the ironically different uses of its space point out the curious choreography of history and of production of space. From a pleasure palace, 'each room in the villa represented a different season,' where the great artists met to a nunnery (from an abode of the pleasures of the senses to a place that kept its inmates away from the carnal desires), from a house of the soldiers to a place of treatment of their victims, the space of the villa undergoes multiple transformations as its occupants and the purposes of occupation change. The villa further becomes the temporary home of the nomads – the patient, Hana, Caravaggio and Kip. The space of the villa never remains static, it is charged up with each new occupant, the old order is revised with every entrance, stay and exit.

A sense of history pervades the place. As if the dismantled state of the villa has not only dismantled the boundaries of space, between the villa and the landscape, but also of time. The villa is at once ancient and modern caught up in a complex web of the ironies of history and the acts of civilisation. So while back in the fifteenth century there were 'the Medicis considering a balustrade or window, holding up a candle at night in the presence of an invited architect' (33) there is the patient, Hana, Kip and Caravaggio right in the middle of the twentieth century moving in the darkness, a house lit only by candles. While in the fifteenth century the great artists argued beside the bust of Plato all night, there is now the patient and Hana reading books late into the night. The past and the present stand together in a close embrace, their complex architectures coincide with the curious choreography of time and deliberate interventions.

The past and the present find their way into each other both in terms of mutual reflections and subtle interventions into its architecture. Pianos, libraries, murals, trompe l'oeils, trees reflect the deliberate playing of present with the seeming innocence of the past, using it as a kind of mask:

> The retreating army often left pencil mines within musical instruments. Returning owners opened up pianos and lost their hands. People would revive the swing on a grandfather clock, and a glass bomb would blow out half a wall and whoever was nearby … . Bombs were attached to taps, to the spines of books, they were drilled into fruit trees so an apple falling on the lower branch would detonate the tree, just as a hand gripping that branch would. (75)

So Kip hanging by the ceiling of the villa's library 'against the trompe l'oeil' (74) trying to diffuse a bomb is another artist in a strange juxtaposition with the works of the two earlier artists, the one from the past who made the painting and the other more contemporary who thought of hiding a bomb there. It is an understanding of this choreography of war that makes Kip 'unable to look at a room or field without seeing the possibilities of weapons there' (75). Kip is able to trace the hidden lines and does not trust what meets the eye, not even the past, his eyes penetrate into the hidden *possibilities*. There is a subtle connection between the perception of Kip and that of the patient. While Kip can sense the hidden threats in the immediate landscape, the patient can sense hidden connections between the layers of history. Both, in different ways, search for hidden possibilities, certain that they exist.

As with the villa there are other spaces with a pervasive sense of history in and around them. The vast stretches of the deserts, that Almásy travelled in his expeditions and charted with his companions, had had others explorers in the past, Herodotus and even much earlier than him there were those who took the same routes. Almásy was credited for the discovery of the lost oasis Zerzura, but his sense of history makes him see the conceit of taking such credits, the conceit of the white eye 'the first step by a white man across a great river, the first sight (by a white eye) of a mountain that has been there forever' (141). So what Almásy does is to rediscover, it's an achievement not of claiming a place for the first time but of stepping into its intimate web of historical discoveries, of stepping into its civilisation:

> I was walking not in a place where no one had walked before but in a place where there were sudden, brief populations over the centuries – a fourteenth century army, a Tebu caravan, the Senussi raiders of 1915. And in between these times – nothing was there. When no rain fell the acacias withered, the wadis dried out ... until water suddenly reappeared fifty or hundred years later. Sporadic appearances and disappearances, like legends and rumours through history. (141)

However, Almásy's sense of history stretches farther back than the medieval or modern discoveries of the desert routes and scattered oases in it. He knows what meets the eye as a desert today was something else completely thousands of years ago and there are clues to this overlooked past all over the place. The desert too has undergone a journey from its ocean space to the vast stretches of sand where 'water became the exile':

> In the desert it is easy to lose a sense of demarcation. When I came out of the air and crashed into the desert, into those troughs of yellow, all I kept thinking was, I must build a raft.
>
> ... I must build a raft.
>
> And here, though I was in the dry sands, I was among water people.
>
> In Tassili I have seen rock engravings from a time when Sahara people hunted water horses from reed boats. In Wadi Sura I saw caves whose walls were covered with paintings of swimmers. Here there had been a lake. I could draw its shape on a wall for them. I could lead them to its edge, six thousand years ago. (18)

Thus the space of the desert contains much more than the ever-shifting patterns of sand. To a historically perceptive eye – even today the caravans look like a river. Still, today it is water who is the stranger her. Water is the exile, carried back in cans and flasks, the ghost between your hands and your mouth. (19)

Along with the vast stretches of the deserts and the limited architectural spaces of villas and churches, Ondaatje uses body as a space. There is a heightened consciousness of body in its textures, structures, scars, the intimate spaces within it and how an individual relates to the space of his or her body, the physicality of his or her existence and relationships. As Hana sits in the fountain of the villa she 'smells her skin, the familiarity of it. One's own taste and flavour' (92). The English patient for Hana is 'A man with no face. An ebony pool' (48). While Kip appears unconsciously in love with his body, Caravaggio is always concerned with his lost balance. As Hana lies beside Kip, she feels the space of his body:

> She likes to lay her face against the upper reaches of his arm, that dark brown river, and to wake submerged within it, against the pulse of an unseen vein in his flesh beside her. The vein she would have to locate and insert a saline solution into if he were dying. (125)

The body of Kip becomes a river for Hana in her intensity of love for him. She 'imagines all of Asia through the gestures of this one man. The way he lazily moves, his quiet civilization' (217). Love produces a desire to know the other in all the spaces of body, history, belonging, aspirations, skills, weaknesses and togetherness. Love opens a curious choreography of time and space; Hana struggles to find a key to Kip:

> She cannot see his order and discipline without seeing his eyes. There isn't a key to him. As if organs, the heart, the rows of rib, can be seen under the skin, saliva across her hand now a colour. He has mapped her sadness more than any other. Just as she knows the strange path of love he has for his dangerous brother. (270)

Similarly, when Kip asks for stories about Toronto 'what he was really interested in were clues to Hana's nature (268), motivated by a desire to know her better. Almásy finds it difficult to put off Katharine's body from his mind even as he writes his own book *Recentes Explorations dans le Desert Libyque*, 'as I wrote my brief book, seventy pages long, succinct and to the point, complete with maps of travel. I was unable to remove her body from the page. I wished to dedicate the monograph to her, to her voice, to her body that I imagined rose white out of a bed like a long bow, but it was a book I dedicated to a king' (235).

Desire translates the space of the body into the book. Love and tenderness for the other make even personal histories susceptible, they open the spaces of personal histories and become tokens, the gifts of the present for the future. The 'vaccination scar' on Katharine's shoulder opens up the space of her childhood for Almásy and he does not simply imagine her in her childhood but gets right into it, 'I see the instrument scratch and then punch the serum within her and then release itself, free of her skin, years ago, when she was nine years old, in a school gymnasium' (150). Almásy holds a belief, 'When we meet those we fall in love with, there is an aspect of our spirit that is historian, a bit of a pedant, who imagines or remembers a meeting when the other had passed by innocently' (259).

Hana too accompanies Kip to the space of his birth, 'During the verbal nights, they travel his country of five rivers. The Sutlej, Jhelum, Ravi, Chenab, Beas. He guides her into the great gurdwara, removing her shoes, watching as she washes her feet, covers her head' (270–271). And when Kip saves Caravaggio by scooping a bomb in middle distance, Caravaggio realizes, 'He could walk away, never see him again, and he would never forget him. Years from now on a Toronto street Caravaggio will get out of a taxi and hold the door open for an East Indian who is about to get into it, and he will think of Kip then' (208).

Like the other spaces in Ondaatje, the body too is embedded with history. The English patient's black burnt body, Caravaggio's lost thumbs, Kip's characteristic brownness of his continent, Hana's leanness and the lost child are histories impressed and imprinted not only in their psyche and memory but on their bodies too. Body becomes a site, a space where time leaves its marks as the body travels through age, love, tortures, violence and passions. While Caravaggio has 'the cluster of known scars on him' (27), the scars that he has received, and the thumbs that had been chopped off in the war, the English patient has also, in his love affair with Katharine acquired a pattern of scars:

> A list of wounds. The various colours of the bruise – bright russet leading to brown. The plate she walked across the room with, flinging its contents aside, and broke across his head, the blood rising up into the straw hair. The fork that entered the back of his shoulder, leaving its bite marks the doctor suspected were caused by a fox. (153)

The leanness of Hana, her face 'without the mystery of long hair' and her sadness are traces from war, personal loss that she bears on her body. Kip in his self-sufficiency, discipline and mechanism of a machine carries the history of his otherness and the constant struggle of his profession to defy death, to neutralise it in the womb of bombs.

Almásy cradles a deep belief in the manifestations of history on the body, the cartography of time on physical space:

> We die containing a richness of lovers and tribes, tastes we have swallowed, bodies we have plunged into and swum up as if rivers of wisdom, characters we have climbed into as if trees, fears we have hidden in as if caves. I wish for all this to be marked on my body when I am dead. I believe in such cartography – to be marked by nature, not just to label ourselves on a map like the names of rich men and women on buildings. We are communal histories, communal books. (261)

Almásy attempts such cartography on Katharine's dead body in the Cave of Swimmers, he 'looked up to the one cave painting and stole the colours from it. The ochre went into her face, he daubed blue around her eyes ... Hoops of colour around her legs so she would be immune to the human. There were traditions he had discovered in Herodotus in which old warriors celebrated their loved ones by locating and holding them in whatever world made them eternal – a colourful fluid, a song, a rock drawing' (248). With the cartography of nature on her body Katharine becomes a part of nature, the colours spread in the landscape. Moments before the crash of Almásy into the desert, the body of Katharine starts disappearing into the sky from the broken cockpit of the plane: She collapses – acacia twigs, leaves, the branches that were shaped into arms uncoiling around him. Limbs begin disappearing in the suck of air ... The woman translated into leaves and twigs, the broken glass to the sky like a jaw above him (175).

After his crash into the desert Almásy himself is marked by cartography of nature by the Bedouin, not so much to immortalise him but to save his life, to heal his burns. The tribe covered him 'with a mask of oasis reeds knitted together. He now had a bearing of grass' (9), the ointments that had 'an odour of the sea. The smell of rust. Indigo. Ink. River-mud arrow-wood formaldehyde paraffin ether, ground peacock bone' (10); they all become parts of the English patient's body and later on in the hospitals, 'Parts of his burned body and face that had been sprayed with tannic acid, that hardened into a protective shell over his raw skin' (48). Every stage of the treatment translates the patient's body into patterns of enigmatic layers of medicine and nature, the body becomes a physical manifestation of the complex layers of the patient's character, protected by the hard shell and the patient's disavowal of names.

Music too is a space, has a structure like a human body, and when played it opens the spaces of the past, extends the present and allows the spaces of the past and future to surface. Hana, at one point, feels claustrophobic in the villa; she opens the doors and lets in night air, goes to the piano that she has never played during her entire stay in the villa. Without looking down 'she lowered her hands and started to play, just chording sound, reducing melody to a skeleton. She paused after each set of notes as if bringing her hands out of water to see what she had caught, then continued, placing down the main bones of the tune' (63). Hana plays on and the song taught by her mother comes back to her and along with it the space of the childhood, the kitchen table where her mother wrote the notes and wiped them later, the myth of the dwarfs told to her by her father, the dwarfs that drank only at the pianos and her belief that the water in the pianos was perhaps drank by the mice, the space of memory is opened by the music.

As Hana swings into her childhood with the swirl of the music, the two sappers enter the villa and stand right in front of her. Hana sees them in a flash of lightening but she plays on carried into the past of the villa told to her by the patient, she considers the possibility, 'What would Poliziano have thought of this 1945 tableau, two men and a woman across a piano and the war almost over … and the music antiphonal, the press of chords, *when I take my sugar to tea* …' (63–64). Further, the initial tentativeness of Hana goes, the bones of the tune start to put on flesh, veins, blood she 'broke free of the chords and released her fingers into intricacy, tumbling into what she had held back, the jazz detail that split open notes and angles from the chestnut of melody … her hands playing now against and within the lightening and thunder, counter to it, filling up the darkness between light' (63–64). The space of music never remains static, the same songs, tunes, notes at different moments of life acquire a different colour, become vehicles of struggles, pains, desires, maps of the self and the other.

Other forms of art too have their spaces and subtle marks of time on them. All through the novel paintings, trompe l' oeils, drawings, murals and statues have a consistent presence. These works of art do not remain in the backdrop or a fete for the aesthetic eye, but they open their spaces to reflect the present and the past in a curious web of relationships. They offer contrasts, striking similarities between the past and the present, art and life and extend their embrace to provide comfort, sleep and solace as everything human around them collapses. The villa has its rooms with a different season painted on the walls of each room. The stillness of the seasons on the walls, the trees, foliage and flowers loses its stasis with the dismantled walls that reveal the garden outside the villa, the sun, the moon, the stars and the showers of rain, the painted gardens extend into real gardens and in different lights reveal different patterns.

Hana at one moment enters the patient's room and sees, 'Moonlight across the foliage on the walls. This was the only light that made the trompe l' oeil seem convincing. She could pluck the flower and pin it onto her dress' (31). Kip was among the troops when a thirteenth century castle was taken by the Allies. The troops billeted under the high dome of the church meet their mythical counterparts:

> Looking up with service binoculars the soldiers would come upon their contemporary faces in the Piero della Francesca frescoes. The Queen of Sheba conversing with King Solomon. Nearby a twig from the Tree of Good and Evil inserted in the mouth of dead Adam. Years later this Queen would realize that the bridge over the Siloam was made from the wood of this sacred tree. (70)

The faces from myths in the intensity of the depicted moment become contemporary. The Queen of Sheba fascinates Kip. Later struggling in a muddy river Kip feels a desire to touch the 'texture of her skin' and the desire 'somehow kept him warm'. Kip's sudden attraction for the painting is a manifestation of his craving for character. Art offers Kip a character, a story, a situation, the mystery of an expression and the certainty how the fate of Queen of Sheba would unfold, the certainty of her future knowledge of the sacredness of bridges, things that Kip himself could not be certain about with the war around him. Though later on he discovers his Queen of Sadness in Hana and the wise King Solomon in the English patient. Something that offers him, like the painting, if not the certainty of fates, character, a story, a situation, a quest to plunge in to know the mystery of Hana's sadness to bring her out of it and in the process redeeming his own loneliness and the sadness induced by the war.

During the entire period of the war Kip found statues in churches to be his sentinels for the nights, 'He had given his trust only to this race of stones, moving as close as possible against them in the darkness, a grieving angel whose thigh was a woman's perfect thigh, whose line and shadow appeared so soft. He would place his head on the lap of such creatures and release himself into sleep'

(104). Hana sleeping beside Kip sees in him such an angel; an angel that could offer her sleep, angel whose tent appeared to be his khaki wings the bone to which Hana tries to touch. The English patient too is an angel for Hana 'the despairing saint' who needed her beside him, to care for him. Later the English patient and Hana see Kip as a 'warrior saint', a saint that had come to protect them from harm.

As Kip leaves the group every morning to attend to his dangerous profession of diffusing bombs Hana is reminded of a mural that she had seen in Siena:

> A fresco of a city. A few yards outside the city walls the artist's paint had crumbled away, so there was not even the security of art to provide an orchard in the far acres for the traveller leaving the castle. That was where, she felt, Kip went during the day. Each morning he would step from the painted scene towards dark bluffs of chaos. The Knight. The warrior saint. (273)

Art unfolds into life; Kip becomes the Knight in the painting leaving the castle each day to counter the chaos that surrounds it. Kip on an earlier occasion, clearing out the mines in the deserted city Naples, with the very likely possibility that they would be blown up with the turning on of the lights of the city by the hidden mines laid out by the retreating Germans, chooses to die beneath the terra-cotta figures of an angel and a woman in conversation in the damaged Church of *San Giovanni a Carbonara*. He wants to die under the care of 'these parental figures' (280). As he sleeps on he becomes a part of the tableau, the distance of time disappears among them:

> There seems to be no time here. Each of them has selected the most comfortable of positions to forget time. So we will be remembered by others. In such smiling comfort when we trust our surroundings. The tableau now, with Kip at the feet of the two figures, suggests a debate over his fate. The raised terra-cotta arm a stay of execution, a promise of some great future for this sleeper, childlike, foreign-born. The three of them almost at the point of decision, agreement. (280–281)

The juxtaposition of art and life, the disappearing of time, the desire to trust the surroundings tie the angel, the woman and Kip in a complex relationship. It is the desire to escape time in its mortality, to have the certainty of art, to reach a point where there is an agreement between the timelessness of art and the temporality of life.

Ondaatje projects an awareness of space in its surfaces, the intricate patterns of history that lie beneath these surfaces, the stretches, the geographies that each space embraces and the way these spaces stand and open themselves in the context of other spaces. The books too are spaces in this context. There is the cover, the paper, and the intimate print, the physical spaces of the books alongside the spaces bound within their narratives. Hana's pulling out of a book from the villa's library becomes a complex act:

> With a crack of separation, as if it were being dismantled from one single unit, she pulled out *The Last of the Mohicans* and even in this half-light was cheered by the aquamarine sky and lake on the cover illustration, the Indian in the foreground ... . She opened the book. The pages were joined together in a stiff wave. She felt like Crusoe finding a drowned book that had washed up and dried itself on the shore. (12)

The physical appearance of the book is the first step towards an intimacy between the reader and the book. Ondaatje projects an awareness of books passing hands, the gradual erosion and the way they stand in relation with other books in a library stack so the pulling out of a book at one level becomes an act of *dismantling a single unit*. And even before a book is opened there are faint traces of the journey of its physical space through time like the book that Crusoe discovered at the shore of an ocean, the book a mirror of Crusoe, another voyager that like Crusoe holds the delicate traces of its voyage through the ocean with its meanings folded inside. So the patient at one point tells Hana "I am a person who if left alone in someone's home walks to the bookcase, pulls down a volume and inhales it. So history enters us" (18).

Elsewhere Hana sits with a copy of Rudyard Kipling's *Kim*, fascinated as she is by the story of the young boy in India who was tossed from teacher to teacher; she considers the book for a different reason now, for its physical presence:

> The book lay on her lap. She realized that for more than five minutes she had been looking at the porousness of the paper, the

> crease at the corner of page 17 which someone has folded over as a mark. She brushed her hand over its skin. A scurry in her mind like a mouse in the ceiling, a moth on the night window. (7)

Ondaatje incorporates the presence of books, the skins of their pages, the numbers and the creased corners, the physical journeys of the books through times and the hands of readers, beside their plots, stories and landscapes. The moments of unconscious gaze, brushing of the page, leaving little marks for memory, looking up from books, the feeling of the presence of life around the book and its reading – *a scurry in her mind like a mouse in the ceiling* – are little acts involved in the act of reading, the acts that often disappear between the plots of the books and the eyes following their storylines but somehow become a part of the complex architecture of the books and their stories, meanings, like flowers pressed between two pages become a part of them, a fragrance that has to be discerned with the waft of the porousness of the paper and its history.

There are ways in which a book has to be approached. A sense of intimacy between the writer and the reader, the act of writing and the act of reading. Hana learns an important reading lesson from the patient, the way one should approach Kipling:

> Read him slowly, dear girl, you must read Kipling slowly. Watch carefully where the commas fall so you can discover natural pauses. He is a writer who used pen and ink. He looked up from the page a lot. I believe, stared through his window and listened to the birds, as most writers who are alone do. Some do not know the names of birds, though he did. Your eye is too quick and North American. Think about the speed of his pen. What an appalling, barnacled old first paragraph it is otherwise. (94)

Ondaatje's consciousness of the space books, like his sense of history in/of geographical spaces or the architectures of buildings stretches back, to the writer, his pen and ink, the landscape around him and the sound of birds. Ondaatje attempts to capture the experience of reading in its simultaneities, a sensitivity that traces the spirit and the environment that surrounded the author and puts it alongside the subjective response of the reader and the environment that prevails around him. The writer, the book, the reader and their corresponding environments transgress into each other's domains, creating a complex dynamics of mutual influences. This challenges the traditional approach where the author retains the prerogative over the text and its implications, is the giver and the reader is pushed to the periphery, to the receiving end. Ondaatje destabilises the tyranny and the monopoly of the author and the text by opening it to incorporate the reader and his environment. The strategy opens the possibilities of the multiple negotiations of the text and its implications and refurbishes the warmth in the writer-text-reader relationship.

Apart from their presence as physical space, the books play a fundamental role in their narrative underpinnings in *The English Patient*. The books open other spaces and landscapes through their narratives and the paths in the books do not remain contained in their covers. With the opening of the books these paths extend their scope into the paths of the present, the paths of the readers and their lives. So when Hana 'begins a book she enters through stilted doorways into large courtyards. Parma, Paris and India spread their carpets' (93) but these exotic landscapes in the course of reading and of time in strange ways find their way into her life as her life enters them – a mutual exchange of character. Kip's entry in the novel and into the lives of the English patient, Hana and Caravaggio has subtle connections with Rudyard Kipling's *Kim*, 'As if the pages of Kipling had been rubbed in the night like a magic lamp' (94); connections that are hinted at in the novel:

> In recent days Hana had watched him sitting beside the English patient, and it seemed to her a reversal of *Kim*. The young student was now Indian, the wise old teacher was English. But it was Hana in the night who stayed with the old man, who guided him over the mountains to the sacred river … . And in some ways on those long nights of reading and listening, she supposed, they had prepared themselves for the young soldier, the boy grown up, who would join them. But it was Hana who was the young boy in the story. And if Kip was anyone, he was the officer Creighton. (111)

Kipling's Kim gets into the narrative and the plot of *The English Patient* in multiple ways. At one point Kirpal Singh the young Indian soldier is Kim in an irony of reversals, at other point Hana becomes Kim, and again Kip and Hana share the role of Kim.

The plot of Kipling's novel exerts its influence in *The English Patient,* and the plot of *The English Patient* has a counter influence on *Kim,* opening it to a contemporary situation.

Ondaatje frequently returns to *Kim, The Charterhouse of Parma* and *The Last of the Mohicans* in the novel. However, closely akin to Ondaatje's approach towards history and the organisation of his narrative is the role that he assigns to the *The Histories* of Herodotus in the novel. *The Histories* of Herodotus, finds significant underpinnings in the text of the novel. The English patient in his miraculous escape from the plane on fire manages to keep *The Histories* that has always accompanied him in the past safe and now lies beside his bed in the villa. The 1890 edition of the book has undergone several transformations. The English patient has used it like a notebook, writing his own observations in the empty spaces within the book, gluing pages from other books:

> She picks up the notebook that lies on the small table beside his bed. It is the book he brought with him through the fire-copy of *The Histories* by Herodotus that he has added to, cutting and gluing in pages from other books or writing in his own observations – so they all are cradled within the text of Herodotus. (16)

The Histories of Herodotus becomes a notebook in the hands of the English patient and the novel in the hands of Michael Ondaatje becomes another notebook, a cradle, where *The Histories* and other books are inserted, glued added to the narrative strand and in fact these alternative and added voices form a curious relationship among themselves become the narrative. The English patient's attachment to the book has a specific reason, a reason that is crucial for the novel as well. The patient tells Hana:

> I have seen editions of *The Histories* with a sculpted portrait on the cover. Some statue found in a French museum. But I never imagine Herodotus this way. I see him more as one of those spare men of the desert who travel from oasis to oasis, trading legends as if it is the exchange of seeds, consuming everything without suspicion, piecing together a mirage. 'This history of mine,' Herodotus says, 'has from the beginning sought out the supplementary to the main argument.' What you find in him are *cul-de-sacs* within the sweep of history – how people betray each

> other for the sake of nations, how people fall in love … . (118–119)

Herodotus, in his emphasis on the power of the supplementary argument, sounds like a postmodern writer, he deals with history in its pluralities and multiplicities, as it slips into *cul-de-sacs*, digresses into legends and myths, suspecting nothing and this way he spatialises the grand linear narrative of homogeneous historical accounts, opening them with an imposition of simultaneities. Ondaatje's technique also comes close to that of Herodotus, he too believes in the power of the supplementary argument, his text holds together the little *cul-de-sacs* of life – acts, characters, and situations – within the sweep of history.

The insertions made into Herodotus's *Histories* by the English patient have different implications – at times they are stray observations put into empty spaces, at other times they are put into specific spaces as they have a clear connection with the narrative of *The Histories* as if Herodotus himself might have included them; at other times *The Histories* becomes a record of the present moment and its struggles. The English patient undergoing a painful phase in his relationship with Katharine Clifton makes an insertion into *The Histories*:

> He bought pale brown cigarette papers and glued them into sections of *The Histories* that recorded wars that were of no interest to him. He wrote down all her arguments against him. Glued into the book – giving himself only the voice of the watcher, the listener, the "he". (172)

The personal wars against the wars of the civilisation, the juxtaposition opens up both the personal and the public histories in their magnitudes and limitations. Life finds an entrance in the text of histories and sometimes the books extend their embrace into life. Hana aligns herself to the patient, not ready to leave him though everyone leaves the villa she stays with the patient, taking care of him and this association of the young nurse with a dying man finds a strange reflection in one of the insertions made by the patient in *The Histories* of Herodotus; as if the plot of the myth has entered their lives. Hana reads a thin paper from the Bible, torn and glued into the book:

> *King David was old and stricken in years and they covered him in clothes but he received no heat.*
>
> *Whereupon his servants said, Let there be sought for the King a young virgin: and let her cherish him, and let her lie in this bosom, that our King may have heat.*
>
> *So they sought for a fair damsel throughout all the coasts of Israel, and found Abishag a Shunammite. And the damsel cherished the King, and ministered to him: but the King knew her not.* (94–95)

Why and when did the patient make this insertion into the book is not hinted at in the novel, but whatsoever the purpose or occasion, Biblical King David and his nurse Abishag find their counterparts in the English patient and the nurse Hana in the twentieth century Italy.

Similarly, the story of Almásy, Katharine Clifton and Geoffrey Clifton becomes a reenactment, an extension of the story of Candaules, his wife and Gyges. In the story Candaules, obsessed with the beauty of his wife, in his vanity, asks Gyges to see her undressing, he makes the necessary arrangements but while Gyges looks at the queen she comes to know of his presence, and gives him two options, either to kill the king and marry her or to die himself; Gyges makes the first choice and slays the king. The story somehow manages to get itself in the lives of Clifton, Katharine and Almásy:

> There are several things one can say. Knowing that eventually I would become her lover, just as Gyges will be the queen's lover and murderer of Candaules. I would often open Herodotus for a clue to geography. But Katharine had done that as a window to her life … . This is a story of how I fell in love with a woman, who read me a specific story from Herodotus. I heard the words she spoke across the fire, never looking up, even when she teased her husband. Perhaps she was just reading it to him. Perhaps there was no ulterior motive in the selection except for themselves. It was simply a story that had jarred her in its familiarity of situation. But a path suddenly revealed itself in real life. (233)

While Almásy uses *The Histories* for clues to *geography*, Katharine uses it as a *window* to her life and the path of the story in *The Histories* reveals itself in *real life*. Ondaatje's incorporation of history in his books is a conscious strategy to dislodge the tyranny of singular historical determinations. In the process of his treatment history melts into the mythical, historical accuracy gives way to the truth of fiction, and the search for specific identities sublimates into the search for character and the specific historical situations transcend to human situations, an act that links the temporal with the timeless.

As with the *The Histories* of Herodotus and Almásy's various insertions into it, those that are precisely related to the narrative of Herodotus, those that reflected the contradictory opinions and those that were random insertions made by him to counteract the flow of the narrative or the need to establish a contact with it in the present. Hana too takes up the habit of writing into books and her insertions precisely reflect the nature of those made by the patient. On three occasions she writes into the spaces of the books – first about Caravaggio on the blank page at the back of *The Last of the Mohicans* (61); second about the *Zam-Zamah* cannon in Lahore made by the melting down of cups and bowls from Hindu households as a tax *jizya* and used in battles against the Sikhs, in the flyleaf in the last pages of Kipling's *Kim* (118); and the last in the empty space between two sections of a volume of poetry about Lahore, London and Canada, about Kip and his charming smile, his being the warrior saint and the thirteen gates of Lahore (209). On the first two occasions the choice of the books is deliberate and on the last Hana closes her eyes and picks up a book at random.

On the first two occasions after writing she hides the books in some invisible corners of the library shelf. Hana's insertions into these books, even as she hides them, establish a relationship between her life and the narratives of these books, she sees reflections of Caravaggio in *The Last of the Mohicans* and Kip in *Kim* and even her act of writing about Kip in a volume of poetry speaks of her love for him, the desire in her to know the home space of Kip. Her poem for him finds a place amid other poems and will probably be read with wonder by a future reader. In Ondaatje intertextuality is not merely at the level of underpinnings of plots of other books and stories, the similarities and contrasts, limitations and extensions but the intertext acquires a broader significance, a complex net of relationships.

The English Patient at one level is a metafiction, where a diverse range of other books – histories, novels, myths, legends, stories and the Bible, intersect and interact with each other with/within the plot of the novel. Ondaatje opens up the boundaries between fact and fiction, private and public, historical and the mythic, ancient and the contemporary, art and life, temporal and the timeless; converting his novel into a constantly evolving ground of consistent negotiations. But as there is a strong element of intertextuality in the novel, and there are multiple stories intersecting with each other in time and space, there is the problem of order and the problem of self-reflexivity of the text brought in through its inclusion of and negotiations with other texts. Here too, Ondaatje does not limit himself to a negotiation with other texts and their stories at a thematic level but on the other hand he negotiates form and order of his own text with them:

> Many books open with an author's assurance of order. One slipped into their waters with a silent paddle .... But novels commenced with hesitation or chaos. Readers were never fully in balance. (93)

In the Skin of a Lion, also expresses this concern with order and form and with the genre of novels. Ondaatje writes: 'The first sentence of every novel should be: "Trust me, this will take time but there is order here, very faint, very human"' (146). *The English Patient* makes a similar demand on its readers, as it moves with its multiple stories and intertexts; the books within the book which do not limit themselves to the referential but come alive within the text of the novel caught up in a relationship of mutual influences.

Ondaatje uses intertextuality as a narrative strategy to undermine linearity, a strategy that helps him to spatialise history in its simultaneities. As Hana opens up books and reads from them to the English patient or to herself, the emphasis is never on the beginnings but it can be any page from any book. The English patient too picks up parts from Hana's reading alongside his own narratives or at other times remains oblivious to them. None of them insist on following the storyline:

> She was not concerned with the Englishman as far as the gaps in plot were concerned. She gave no summary of the missing

chapters. She simply brought out the book and said "page ninety-six" or "page one hundred and eleven". That was the only locator. (8)

Much in the nature of the Holy Book, the *Guru Granth Sahib* that is 'opened at random, a quotation selected, and for three hours, before the mist lifts off the lake to reveal the Golden Temple, the verses mingle and sway out with unbroken reading' (271). Each time there is a new beginning, the verses deriving their strength from their spirit rather than their linearity.

Hana opens and closes the books or leaves them open, immerses herself into their worlds or looks up from them. Life intervenes and the narrative of the books cannot be carried any further, but even the plot of their lives in the seemingly detached world of the villa, is disturbed by 'the occasional thunder or lightning' coming from nature or an explosion nearby. Similarly, the English patient's accounts of his desert expeditions and his love story with Katharine Clifton are repeatedly interrupted by the readings from the books, the small incidents that take place around him or with the arrival of new characters in the story. Michael Greenstein in his "Ondaatje's Metamorphoses: In the Skin of a Lion", points out, "interception and interruption characterize two ways of proceeding through Ondaatje's text: narrative pushes the reader forward while lyrical imagery turns around on itself. The latter move involves a typically postmodernist self-reflexivity, which constantly draws attention to the boundaries within which the writer, reader and character alike are operating" (*Canadian Literature*, No. 126, Autumn, 1990: 116–30).

An analysis of the various spaces in Ondaatje reveals a characteristic commonality in them. Landscapes, buildings, books, bodies, paintings and music reveal certain common influences. Each of these spaces undergoes constant transformations. The agencies of these transformations are the same, and it is at this point of multiple erosions caused by private, public and natural histories that the boundaries of these spaces open to each other and extend their grasps to reflect other spaces and times. Therefore, rooms become landscapes, books translate themselves into characters and the bodies become books, communal histories, sadness has a map and there is the sadness of geography, the desert has the architecture of morphine and morphine becomes a space, a country with its citizens of morphia. Maps become bodies and bodies are mapped by the traces of their histories. Paintings and statues unfold into life and life itself becomes a part of their tableaus.

From the narrative standpoint the transgression/melting of one space into others and one time into other times performs a crucial function. Ondaatje's narrative moves in a circular manner catching up with the temporal and spatial turns. The juxtapositions of the different spaces and times and the constantly blurred borders make them self-reflexive and this self-reflexivity becomes Ondaatje's governing narrative strategy. The spaces in their corrosions reflect each other and Ondaatje's narrative structure bears a close resemblance to them. For instance, the plots of the books that Hana reads to the English patient resemble the dilapidated the villa:

> So the books for the Englishman, as he listened intently or not, had gaps of plot like sections of a road washed out by storms, missing incidents as if locusts had consumed a section of tapestry, as if plaster loosened by the bombing had fallen away from a mural at night.
>
> The villa that she and the Englishman inhabited now was much like that. Some rooms could not be entered because of rubble. One bomb crater allowed moon and rain into the library downstairs – where there was in one corner a permanently soaked armchair. (7–8)

The structuring of *The English Patient* is in the nature of the crumbling architecture of the villa, a simultaneous coexistence of the patterns of order and chaos, mystery and clarity. The shifts in the narrative remain unpredictable like in the villa Hana 'would open a door and see just a sodden bed huddled against a corner, covered with leaves. Doors opened into landscape. Some rooms had become an open aviary' (13). What meets the eye may cause a sudden surprise but once discovered it falls into order, becomes a part of the complex structure. Even the most sudden of the narrative departures can be traced back to their points of origin and are more in the nature of narrative extensions into different directions that can move back and forth in time and space.

The novel at the centre remains a poem, a poetic image melting into multiple poetic images that in all their distinctiveness convey an integrated tone. Ironically, Ondaatje achieves this effect by presenting times, spaces, characters and architectures as they go through disintegration. Ondaatje depicts humanity and its contradictory creations of war and art in its most vulnerable moments where nothing can remain static and secluded or solitary. Ondaatje's narrative achievement comes close to Terry Eagleton's concept of the narrative task:

> To 'deconstruct', then, is to reinscribe and resituate meanings, events and objects within broader movements and structures; it is, to speak, to reverse the imposing tapestry in order to expose in all its unglamorously disheveled tangle the threads constituting the well heeled image it presents to the world. (qtd. by Soja, 12)

Ondaatje deconstructs the *imposing tapestry* of settled historical and spatial determinations by situating them in a state of crisis, and through their juxtaposition in their vulnerabilities *reinscribes and resituates meanings* and relationships within the broader context of humanity.

In the treatment of the different spaces Ondaatje shows a characteristic inclination towards *cul-de-sacs*, the random time capsules that survive the erosions of man and nature. The crucial aspect of these random time capsules is that within their space they embrace the unhistorical lives and traces of different times. They offer no simple pattern and their beauty lies in the complexity of their association. There are such spaces in the desert in the forms of oasis that bear the traces of their histories of being oceans. Almásy says that the desert is a place of pockets. The villa in the novel is another pocket within the space of the war, a space that holds within itself the traces of the past and the present in a complex order and within the villa, there is the oval shaped library, the alcove of the window in the English patient's room which is inhabited alternately by Hana and Kip, the dried fountain outside the villa with its cool moth smell of stone, a place where Hana curls herself in and is somehow liked by Caravaggio too.

Even within the books there are these pockets made by intimate insertions in them and at times the plot too offers such pools, the pools that can be returned to and stayed. The bodies also have such spots the clift on the skin just below the rib, the indentation in the neck that the English patient is taken in by, the 'bohosporous hug.' In music there are the burdens with their little parlours and statues have their laps that offer comfort of sleep. All these spaces lie within the structure of the larger and smaller spaces, and are a part of them but somehow have an intimacy that the main structures do not offer.

These spaces can be compared to the Foucauldian notions of heterotopias – the places that bring together and juxtapose the otherwise contradictory spaces. They are not utopias as these spaces are real, as real as the space within which they lie. The villa in *The English Patient* is such a heterotopia where the different stages of the history of the villa along with the history of Italy and the present erosions of war and the strange ensemble of unlikely inhabitants juxtaposes different histories, cultures, identities in mutually influencing and negotiating relationships.

The desert is another heterotopia in its civilisation of the ever-shifting patterns of sand and its past civilisation of the oceans that survive miraculously in the oases in it. The desert does not have the boundaries in the sense in which they exist in nation states. Almásy and the other desert explorers took to the desert in the intermediate years between the two wars. They escaped into the borderless desert at a time when the nations around them were intruding into their neighbouring territories and colonial states, fought for what they presumed belonged to them. These are 'men of all nations' those 'who like Conrad's sailors, are not too comfortable with the etiquette of taxis, the quick, flat wit of bus conductors' (133). They cling to their maps and lecture notes and enter the city in the evenings, 'an anonymous time', for the lectures in the Geographical Society. They were not simply English or European, while they belonged to different nations, the group itself was 'a small clutch of a nation between the wars, mapping and re-exploring', (136) a nation that had its own culture, and citizens who despite their different nationalities held a common faith in layers of civilisation rather than its surfaces and believed in the ever shifting borders of the desert, knew the necessity of moving like the sands because 'if you pause sand builds up as it would around anything stationary, and locks you in. You are lost forever' (137).

These men feel themselves 'lost' in the nation states and they are rather more comfortable moving in the moving borders of the desert. As they move into the inner recesses of the desert they lose faith in the nation states. They meet desert tribes ignored by history as the desert itself:

> There were rivers of desert tribes, the most beautiful humans I've met in my life. We were German, English, Hungarian, African – all of us insignificant to them. Gradually we became nationless. I came to hate nations. We are deformed by nation-states. (138)

The distrust of nation-states emerges in the group as a result of their deliberate dislocation from the borders of these nation-states. Their faith in nations is replaced by a faith in the desert. They inhale and internalise the spirit of the desert that defies ownership:

> The desert could not be claimed or owned – it was a piece of cloth carried by winds, never held down by stones, and given a hundred shifting names long before Canterbury existed, long before battles and treaties quilted Europe and the East. Its caravans, those strange rambling feasts and cultures, left nothing behind, not an ember. All of us, even those with European homes and children wished to remove the clothing of our countries. It was a place of faith. (138–139)

Almásy and the other desert explorers learn an important lesson about identity in the desert. Nations become pieces of clothing that can be removed or put on never completely revealing the person within them. The desert's defiance of ownership enters Almásy and the others; like the desert they are not ready to be owned, to be restricted by nations or names. Almásy falls in love with the desire, 'I wanted to erase my name and the place I had come from. By the time war arrived, after ten years in the desert, it was easy for me to slip across borders, not to belong to anyone, to any nation' (139).

Almásy is not ready to be owned even in love (152, 238). Later on Almásy claims to be English, using national signification as a piece of clothing to camouflage his identity. It can be argued that he claimed to be English in order to save himself from political persecution for siding with the Germans during the war. But given his state, the body entirely burnt, he could not have survived either way. So his assumption of English identity is a gesture rooted in his distrust of nation states, it is as true and as false as his Hungarian identity.

War in itself is a heterotopia of political deviation, a space that brings together other spaces and individuals and leaves its marks on them, destroying the distinctions and boundaries between them through a common logic of destruction. War obliterates identity by capturing individuals into a similar situation but even when it is over the individuals cannot simply return to the cocoon of their national identities. Caravaggio, thinking about his past in Canada when 'he slipped through his chosen world with a lazy confidence, brilliant in deceit against the rich, or charm towards his wife Giannetta or with this young daughter of his friend' (40); comes to acknowledge the state in which war has brought them, 'But now there is hardly any world around them and they are forced back on themselves' (40).

On another occasion, sitting in the English patient's room, Caravaggio remembers the deceits used in the war, the way individuals camouflaged their identities or invented agents 'phantoms who would take on flesh' or there were others who 'invented whole platoons in the desert.' It was a time 'when everything offered up to those around him was a 'lie' but with the retreat of the war all its camouflages became insignificant and Caravaggio staying in the villa with others feels – 'But here they were shedding skins. They could imitate nothing but what they were. There was no defence but to look for the truth in others' (117).

They have to, as Caravaggio acknowledges, look for truth in others. Hana in her experience of the war has ceaselessly nursed the patients, the endless bodies with endless wounds she 'swabbed arms that kept bleeding. She removed so many pieces of shrapnel she felt she'd transported a ton of metal out of the huge body of the human that she was caring for while the army travelled north' (50). The distinctions of names, countries, and professions vanish and everyone has one name 'Buddy,' a name that ironically suggested a companionship and a deliberate distance, a neutrality, the impersonal 'Buddy' provided a tentative comfort of remaining unattached in dealing with death. Hana stops looking at herself in the mirrors and once when she inadvertently captures her reflection in a mirror:

> She watched the little portrait of herself as if within a clasped brooch. She. Through the window there was the sound of the patients being brought out into the sunlight in their chairs, laughing and cheering with the staff. Only those who were seriously ill were still indoors. She smiled at that. Hi Buddy, she said. She peered into her look, trying to recognize herself. (52)

Hana becomes unrecognisable to herself, the boundaries between the patients she attends and herself vanish and like them she too is not a name or a face but the neutral 'Buddy'. Identity loses significance, gives way to responsibility and it is only through understanding the 'map of responsibility' that one can hope to come out of war and its overpowering shadows of death. Kip measures himself against the nuclear bomb, imagining ways to diffuse it. Hana learns the virtues of rest as opposed to sleep:

> To rest was to receive all aspects of the world without judgement. A bath in the sea, a fuck with a soldier who never knew your name. Tenderness towards the unknown and the anonymous, which was a tenderness to the self. (49)

A *tenderness* towards the others becomes *a tenderness to the self*. Hana aligns herself to the burnt body and the anonymity of the English patient, curing his body and in the process her spirit broken by the war and the death of her father Patrick:

> She stepped away from the war. She had moved back and forth at their desire. Till the nuns reclaimed it she would sit in this villa with the Englishman. There was something about him she wanted to learn, grow into and hide in, where she could turn away from being an adult. There was some little waltz in the way he spoke to her and the way he thought. She wanted to save him this nameless faceless man who had been one of the two hundred or so placed in her care during the invasion north. (52)

Hana by caring for the English patient cures herself of the pain of not being able to care for her father when he died. The curing is not one-sided, the English patient whom she sees as an 'ebony pool' becomes a real pool for Hana, a pool beside which Hana may sit, grow as if under the love of her own father.

Even Caravaggio who 'avoided permanent intimacies', and who had been 'a man who slips away, in the way lovers leave chaos, the way thieves leave reduced houses' (116) and who as an uncle for Hana 'had been a disappearer' (48); comes to the villa as soon as he hears about Hana. He develops a desire to save her from sadness and in the process assumes the responsibility of being her father. Kip who has learnt to suspect everything in his training as a sapper and who finds it difficult to sleep unless he finds the company of some stone angels, a man who insists on being alone never risking others' lives, himself becomes the protecting saint for the group in the villa; the man in whose arms Hana could release herself into sleep. In return Kip finds another father, a teacher and a friend in the English patient, an uncle in Caravaggio and a lover in Hana. The English patient sees his image as a young man in Kip, he calls him his David and both Caravaggio and the English patient, like fathers or uncles, have a desire to see Hana and Kip married.

The desert, the war and the villa in different ways posit a challenge to nationalistic identities. The desert teaches Almasy to distrust nations and the war with its singular logic of destruction teaches Hana, Kip and Caravaggio to distrust nations. The relationships that the English patient, Hana, Kip and Caravaggio develop are ungoverned by their countries. Each of them is dislocated, the English patient calls himself and Kip 'international bastards' those who were born somewhere and chose to live elsewhere. But the expression holds good even for Hana and Caravaggio and though Caravaggio's country of origin is Italy but now his home is in Canada and he is equally a stranger in Italy. However, the war has dislocated them even further but this dislocation forces them to see the other side of location, of feeling the safety of being located in specific spaces and restricted to certain identities. Caring for each other in the villa they climb above the walls of Canada, India, Italy, England or Hungary they discover the bindings of character by shedding the skins of nationalistic significations.

While the spaces that Ondaatje offers are real, there is a recurrent desire to walk, like Almásy, into a space that has no maps, into the 'millimetre of haze just above the inked fibres of a map, that pure zone between land and chart between distances and legend between nature and storyteller Here, apart from the odometer mileage and the book, he was alone, his own invention' (246). Though the desert offers such a space to Almásy, the desire remains utopian, as the desert cannot be inhabited forever. At the end of the desert lie the countries with their borders and politics. The nomadic state has its virtues, Hana observes 'this is the world of nomads in any case' but the lines are eventually drawn. Willingly or unwillingly there are sides to be taken. While the historical Almásy sided with the Germans for political reasons Ondaatje's Almásy does it for love.

Nations deform individuals, Madox kills himself, and identities persecute but they cannot be avoided. Thereby Kip who had learnt everything from the white men and who risked his life for their sake can no longer remain in Europe after the dropping of the bomb on Hiroshima and Nagasaki. He knows 'they would never have done it to a white nation'. Kip finds it futile to be in Europe 'fighting English battles' while 'the streets of Asia were full of fire.' He turns with his gun aiming at the English patient, not so much with a desire to kill him but he turns against whatever the English or the white men stand for. The patient dies, Kip returns to India and becomes a doctor, in keeping with his family tradition. Hana and Caravaggio return to Canada. Though eventually identity and the nation states take their toll; draw the dividing lines but Almásy, Hana, Kip and Caravaggio become more human by the experience of togetherness in a state of crisis. By un-aligning them from specific locations Ondaatje realigns their sense of being.

The English Patient proposes a complex dialectic of what Soja refers to as 'time, space and social being.' Ondaatje projects multiple dislocations through the war, the desert and architectures. These dislocations in a way become the testing grounds for the specifics that are operational within different nation states. By dislocating individuals from their specific nations and putting them into a state of crisis Ondaatje attempts to dislodge the tyrannical claims of national significations. It is a situation where the barriers of nations, races, and genders demand to be transcended into a realisation of the human essence of being. By emphasising the depth of character, the felt need for the other and the essential commonality of human suffering over narrow claims of identity, whether nationalistic or otherwise, Ondaatje's text exposes the fragility of rigid conceptions of identity. Almásy's distrust of nation states, the desire of not to be owned touches the raw nerve of expatriate sensibility. The expatriate seeks belonging but walks away from ownership. Ondaatje's use of history and geography reemphasise this belief.

Note

1. Refer to Jain, Jasbir. "Geographical Dislocations and the Poetics of Exile: Ashis Gupta and Michael Ondaatje." *Writers of the Indian Diaspora*. Ed. Jasbir Jain. Jaipur and New Delhi: Rawat Publications, 1998.

Works Cited

Foucault, Michel. "Texts/Contexts: Of Other Spaces." *Diacritics,* Spring 1986.

Greenstein, Michael. "Ondaatje's Metamorphoses: *In the Skin of a Lion*." *Canadian Literature*, No. 126, 116–30 (Autumn, 1990).

Ondaatje, Michael. *In the Skin of a Lion*. Toronto: McClelland and Stewart, 1987.

——. *The English Patient* (1992). Toronto: Vintage Books, 1993.

Soja, Edward W. *Postmodern Geographies*: *The Reassertion of Space in Critical Theory*. Jaipur and New Delhi: Rawat Publications. 1997.

5

The Politics of Exile

> As soon as I *desire* I am asking to be considered. I am not merely here-and-now, sealed into thingness. I am for somewhere else and for something else ... .
>
> I should constantly remind myself that the real *leap* consists in introducing invention into existence.
>
> In the world in which I travel, I am endlessly creating myself. And it is by going beyond the historical, instrumental hypothesis that I will initiate my cycle of freedom.
>
> Frantz Fanon (qtd. by Bhabha, 8)

Fanon's statement has a crucial significance in the politics of exile. The act of *desiring* leads to a speaking out, a manifest assertion of the expatriate's claim to be *considered,* seeking a recognition and empowerment in more complex ways than might be allowed by the static *historical, instrumental hypothesis*. Fanon resists *thingness*, to be locked in *here-and-now* as he locates the essence of being in an openness towards the future whereby he may introduce *invention into existence* and through an exposure to the world in its variousness may *endlessly* create himself. However, going beyond *here-and-now* demands in the first place an approximation of the present in the way as it has come to be through the passage of history and inter-cultural influences.

Bhabha underlines Fanon's emphasis on the 'crucial importance, for subordinated peoples, of asserting their indigenous cultural traditions and retrieving their repressed histories' (Bhabha, 9). The act of retrieval of repressed histories works as an imperative in the context of the historically marginalised groups as it allows them to question the oppressive centre-periphery relationship and to claim for themselves the historically denied position in the power structures in the present. However, the project of retrieval has significance insofar as it does not become a conscious effort to revert to pre-colonial notions of identity or cultural significations. The assertion of silent/silenced histories is not a movement into the past to undo the historical wrong or an exercise of lamentation but its value lies precisely in its potential to influence the present and the settled structures of power.

The poetics of exile has insuperable politics attached to it. The expatriate's act of articulation whether intended or not is political in nature. Dislocation, cultural and geographical, forces the expatriate to take a fresh measure of his being and belonging. The desire to find a sustainable stand in the socio-political structure of the adopted homes is met with a rigorous resistance from the established structures and their politically unacknowledged nevertheless clearly visible hierarchies of discrimination. These structures by denying easy acceptability or conversely through an easy accommodation into the existing slots force the expatriate upon him/herself. The situation induces a crisis whereby the expatriate has to look in and look out, look back and look at his/her existence vis-à-vis the predetermined constricting frames of identification to negotiate a sustainable sense of identity.

Looking back, and to search for one's roots is not a leisurely act of romancing with nostalgia but it reflects an essential stage in the politics of exile. It is a politically potent move, by reclaiming an overlooked past, the expatriate stakes his claim to be considered beyond the constraints of existing frameworks. However, an exploration of the past ties, reassuring as it might seem at a personal level, has its significance in the sense of group solidarity, an anchorage that it offers to the expatriate in both the spaces.

The borders between the private and the public domains are seriously problematised in the expatriate experience. The private becomes the public, through a triangular politicisation – from the mainstream, the immigrant community and the community back in the country of origin. In a way the position of the expatriate is doubly compromised. An effort to reclaim roots or search a belonging in origins runs the risk of stereotypical labelling 'ethnic' and if the expatriate consciously tries to evade 'ethnicity' he/she may become a pariah within his own community for sacrificing his experience of otherness and not voicing the migrant cause. Quite ironically, from another perspective, the position of the expatriate is doubly liberating if he considers the operational constraints facile and preserves his prerogative of reinventing, recasting remolding himself and thus initiating his *cycle of freedom*.

The poetics and politics of exile raise a set of complex issues: how constraining or liberating it is to be an expatriate? Does migration mean a mechanical switching over of allegiances? If not, how does one prioritise? Does assimilation into the adopted culture mean a sacrifice of cultural diversity? How feasible are the establishmentarian 'melting-pots' and 'mosaic' formulations of national cultures? Where does 'culture' develop in a multicultural society: are there spaces between impositions of homogeneity and self-willed isolations of immigrant communities into heterogeneous ghettos? Can there be *authentic* representations of the cultures of origin and of adoption? Whom does the expatriate represent – his own community in the adopted home, the community in the country of origin or can he represent the entire immigrant community? How politically potent are these representations? What are the corresponding obligations and responsibilities towards the countries of adoption and of origin especially when they become conflictual in situations of political crisis?

Michael Ondaatje's poetics addresses the above concerns and issues in multiple ways. From a political perspective his early works *The Collected Works of Billy the Kid*, *Coming Through Slaughter* and the family memóir *Running in the Family* are relatively apolitical in nature though they have an implicit *cultural politics* and have not been without political controversies. Ondaatje's political perspective has a visible manifestation in his later works *In the Skin of a Lion*, *The English Patient* and *Anil's Ghost*.

Ondaatje's renditions of the legendary American outlaw William Bonney in *The Collected Works of Billy the Kid* and Buddy

Bolden the unrecorded but popular New Orleans Black jazz musician in *Coming Through Slaughter* have been received variously. *The Collected Works of Billy the Kid* was critically acclaimed though it triggered an angry response from a politician, John Diefenbaker, a former Prime Minister of Canada, found it grossly inappropriate to confer a Canadian award (the Governor General's Award) to a book written on a non-Canadian subject. He lambasted Ondaatje for his American sympathies by pointing out that even Canadian historical figures were "every bit as colorful as what's-his-name in the coonskin hat" (Jewinski, 83). Ondaatje did not have to do too much in his defense, as there were obvious chinks in Diefenbaker's literary and historical knowledge. Diefenbaker's outburst was definitely ill-grounded though it is difficult to envisage that he could have been the only one to take such a view of the work.

The most significant aspect of Ondaatje's treatment of these semi-historical figures lies in the cultural perspective. Ondaatje appropriates the cultural others and gives himself a kind of mask and a voice that has no ostensible connections with him. While the act may appear transgressive it is not. Ondaatje's choice and confident treatment of these figures speaks of his inheritance of colonial and postcolonial inter-cultural influences. They are not strenuous and self-conscious presentations of the cultural other but on the other hand writing about/as Billy the Kid has a *natural* context in Ondaatje, given his British colonial education and exposure to the American comic books and movie Westerns in his childhood in Ceylon. Again writing about a black Buddy Bolden may raise issues of authentic representation but Ondaatje's treatment reveals a level of comfort. Ondaatje relates to Buddy Bolden on the level of his art and with his own experience of living in England and Canada he is not oblivious of Buddy's cultural context in the 1920s New Orleans.

Ondaatje's turn to Sri Lanka and his family with the memoir *Running in the Family* received serious critical attention. The book has an important place in the evolvement of Ondaatje's politics. For the first time in his writing career Ondaatje attempted to speak about the country and culture of his origin. The book also represents Ondaatje's shift from individual characters to a group or collective existence. Ondaatje has called the book a gesture to his family, something very personal, but given his milieu and recognition the book was gauged through multiple perspectives. A majority of Canadian critics were impressed by Ondaatje's creation of the exoticism of Ceylon and the surrealistic life of his forebears. Balliett Whitney in an early review of the book observed:

> It is a kind of travel book – eloquent, oblique, witty, full of light and feeling – that keeps spilling over into poetry, into fiction, into slapstick and high-class adventure. But it is only partly about the heat and mountains and jungles of Ceylon. Rather it concentrates on the queer, wild, uncontrollable countries that Lalla and Mervyn turned their lives into. (*The New Yorker*, 27 December, 1982, pp. 76–77)

However, everyone was not approbatory. A strong reaction came from the Indian Canadian critic Arun Mukherjee. Mukherjee was put off by, what she saw as, Ondaatje's exoticist manoeuvres, strategically organised to gratify the adventure-seeking palates of the western audience. Mukherjee in "The Poetry of Michael Ondaatje and Cyril Dabydeen: Two Responses to Otherness" proposes, "Ondaatje's success has been won largely through a sacrifice of his regionality, his past and most importantly, his experience of otherness in Canada." She finds Ondaatje guilty on two accounts, first "there is no trauma of uprooting evident in his poetry" and secondly, "If one were looking for a cross-cultural experience, or a yard-stick against which the "Canadian" writing could be measured in order to isolate the factors that make up its Canadianness, one would be equally disappointed." Mukherjee finds *Running in the Family* equally elliptical. Quoting Raymond Williams' words on Trollope, Mukherjee sees a relevant context in Ondaatje's *Running in the Family*: "What is seen in a social structure with pastoral trimmings. The agricultural poor are placed easily between the produce and the pleasures. And while this easy relationship holds, there is no moral problem of any consequence to disturb the smooth and recommending construction." Mukherjee emphasises a similar relationship in Ondaatje's portrayal of Sri Lanka in *Running in the Family*. She drives home the conclusion, "Ondaatje's unwillingness or inability to place his family in a network of social relationships makes the book a collection of anecdotes which may or may not be funny depending on one's own place in the world" (*Journal of Canadian Literature*. 20, No. I, Spring, 1985: 49–67).

Mukherjee's criticism opens a valid perspective in a critical assessment of the poetics of exile from the standpoint of socio-cultural and political allegiances and authentic cultural representations. However, the problem lies in an easy generalisation or the imposition of a homogeneous order on the poetics and the politics of exile. In this context the remarks of Renee Green may prove particularly instructive:

> Even then, it's still a struggle for power between various groups within ethnic groups about what's being said and who's saying what, who is representing who? What is a community anyway? What is a black community? What is a Latino community? I have trouble with thinking of all these things as monolithic fixed categories. (qtd. by Bhabha, 3)

The questions Green raises open the dynamics of political empowerment in the context of the marginalised communities. There are operational hierarchies and inherent heterogeneity within the narrowest definitions of communities and cultures. While Green finds it difficult to envisage a community as a *monolithic fixed category*, similarly Third World immigrant community cannot be apprehended as a homogenous entity. The trauma/s of dislocation differ and so too the socio-cultural backgrounds and the positions in the adopted homes. It is only in a broad general sense to have a sense of group solidarity that the community can be seen as a homogenous entity. Otherwise such a view is playing in the hands of the stereotypical modes of determination. Whereby people as different as Cyril Dabydeen (Caribbean Canadian of Indian origin), Michael Ondaatje (Sri Lankan Burgher), Rohinton Mistry (Indian Parsi) or for that matter Arun Mukherjee herself is a 'Paki' to the white eye. A narrow identification of this group means an annihilation of the subtle diversities that foster the creative impulse and its conversion into a community of exile with its own set of *givens* and the parameters of trauma, resistance to discrimination, and common poetic/political goals.

The politics in *Running in the Family* is very subtle and complicated. It brings out precisely the fundamental differences within the narratives of dislocation, the historical backgrounds and sense of belonging. The eccentricities and high class adventure of Ondaatje's forebears puts their community in a precise historical context, in a network of social relationships within the Ceylonese society whereby their alienation is more than visible. Suwanda Sugunasiri in "'Sri Lankan' Canadian Poets: The Bourgeoisie That Fled the Revolution" remarks:

> The drunken escapades of the men and women, eating snakes, breaking the necks of chickens, throttling mongrel dogs, running naked in tunnels are *not* unrepresentative of the Eurasian sub-startum elite ... however decadent, colonial or counterdevelopemental it appears from the national point of view. The characters were celebrating their status – with the scantest of respect for anyone other than themselves. Indeed the Eurasian behaviour of *Running* must be seen as simply the first stage of post-colonial Sri Lankan culture, the later stages of which can be seen in the increasingly consumer-oriented and westernizing contemporary Sri Lanka under capitalism. (*Canadian Literature*, 132, 1992: 60–79)

In fact what Ondaatje does is that he gives quite an accurate picture of the alienation of his community back home. While it is a political statement in itself, it is important to consider how far does Ondaatje subscribes to or identifies himself with the position of his community in the pre-independence era of Sri Lanka. What options are available to him as he looks back to grasp the hybridity of his community and his own emotional ties? In the historical context Ondaatje did not have too many options. His community and family did belong to the economic elite of the country, but does that necessarily mean that he should be apologising for his community and his own belonging to it? How should he be apologising – as one of the colonisers or the colonised – as he partakes from both? Can such an apology suffice? And what do these historical relations mean anyway in the present, in the Canadian context?

All these questions are important and Ondaatje's *Running in the Family* holds subtle clues to their answers. Ondaatje's portrayal of his family is neither celebratory nor apologetic but it contextualises his family and community from a socio-cultural and historical perspective. The tone of excess and casualness of

Running in the Family is Ondaatje's effort to recuperate the excesses and irresponsibility of his parents' generation. The description of Sri Lankan landscape in the travelogue has brought in the charges of exociticism on Ondaatje. However, this view demands a closer consideration. Graham Huggan in "Exoticism and Ethnicity in Michael Ondaatje's *Running in the Family*" points out the implicit irony in Ondaatje's exoticist description of the Sri Lankan landscape that 'mocks his readers and himself for playing the part of wide-eyed foreigners.' Huggan remarks, "By mediating his experiences of Sri Lanka through an exoticist "discourse of the other", Ondaatje disengages himself from the very culture he claims to be approaching" (*Essays on Canadian Writing*, No. 57, Winter, 1995: 116–27). But Ondaatje's disengagement from the Sri Lankan culture is partial and in his exoticist discourse can be traced the elements of the exoticism that pulled his first ancestor like many other European voyagers to the island. Ondaatje is in a position of complex socio-cultural allegiances – *I am the foreigner, I am the prodigal who hates the foreigner* – he cannot be anyone but himself.

While Ondaatje partakes from the cultural syncretism of his family, he has to reinvent his relationship with Sri Lanka. He cannot take his relationship with the island for granted and therefore has to negotiate his belonging through the historical relations and his own position for being a foreigner for a substantial part of his life. Therefore Ondaatje simultaneously engages and disengages himself from the Sri Lankan culture. Ondaatje carefully juxtaposes the different perspectives and relationships, that of the imperial invaders, his own ancestors, the voices that he did not know existed and the natives whom his ancestors ignored. The perspectives and relationships with their contradictions coalesce and disperse in *Running in the Family*, and the interstice, the in-between spaces, of contradictions and differences allows Ondaatje, through imaginative appropriation and recreation, situate his own evolving relationship with the island (see Chapter 3).

Ajay Heble underlines Ondaatje's achievement: "Acknowledging both the powers and the limits of its representational activity, the proximity and the distance of Ondaatje's relationship with Sri Lankan culture, *Running in the Family* presents the dialogic mode as a way of modulating from the condition of cultural displacement into a declaration of the possibilities of solidarity" ("Rumours of Topography: The Cultural Politics of Michael Ondaatje's *Running in the Family*". *Essays on Canadian Writing*, No. 53, Summer, 1994: 186–203).

If the politics of *Running in the Family* requires a little digging, the task gets relatively easier with *In the Skin of a Lion* and *The English Patient*. These novels, though not professedly political in nature, have explicit political implications. In both the novels Ondaatje creates multicultural situations and explores the negotiable spaces within and across geo-political and socio-cultural boundaries (refer to Chapters 3 and 4). It is important to notice that a recreation or rewriting of history does not have to be necessarily limited to a communal perspective. Ondaatje recreates the past eras of European and Canadian histories and chooses characters other than those from his own community. Ondaatje's deliberate transgression into the European past and representing the cause of other immigrant communities or dislocated peoples becomes more ex-centric and potent political empowerment of the poetics and politics of exile. The politics in these novels lies in Ondaatje's effort to create human grounds for negotiation of *difference* and search for compensatory affilative evolvement of cultural relationships by going beyond filiative ties.

"The struggle of man against power," says Milan Kundera, "is the struggle of memory against forgetting." To remember, to retrieve, to reenter, to resurface and to reinvent memory is an act of simultaneous annihilation and resurgence of both the individual and collective self, a resistance to the sweeping tyrannies of blinkered history and the power craving body politic, that reduces people to essences, into transparent objects that can be looked through and framed into politically viable categories of racial, religious, regional, and sexual denominations. Memory makes the self opaque, irreducible to a body or geography, an idea or ideology though it carries bodies, geographies, ideas and ideologies within its complex discursive weavings. The narratives of memory have a crucial significance in the constructs of the self and nation and at the same time they bring to the fore the politics, both covert and overt, in the context of the diasporas.

Michael Ondaatje's *In the Skin of a Lion* and Salman Rushdie's *Midnight's Children* can be studied as interesting examples of the diasporic constructs of the self and the nation that open multiple perspectives in the politics of the diaspora at both the individual and communal levels. The two works have a fundamental difference, a difference of vantage points and positions from which their authors enter into personal and collective memories. While Rushdie gets into the history and the margins of the history of his country of origin, India; Ondaatje gets into the skin of histories of his adopted home Canada and explores memories that are not his own. Both Rushdie and Ondaatje make strong claims, claims that are central to their notions of self and claims that have unmistakable socio-cultural and political implications.

There are several questions that need to be addressed: What does the writing of the self entail? Can the writing of the self be limited to personal pasts? Where does the private end and public begin? Can the writing of the self be a writing of the nation? Can one claim memories, histories and pasts other than his or her own? What are the socio-cultural and political implications of such claims? How imaginary are the imaginary homelands? What lies between material and the metaphoric homelands? What are the inherent advantages and compromises of the diasporic and at home writers in their mappings of the self and the nation? Can the migrant's fabled 'double-vision' be treated as the vision?

The poetics of Michael Ondaatje and Rushdie hold subtle clues to these questions. Saleem Sinai in *Midnight's Children* and Patrick Lewis in *In the Skin of a Lion* take a stride into their personal histories and find themselves drawn into a maze of other histories that insist on digressions, that offer counter narratives and subvert homogenising. Fredric Jameson offers an important clue in his notion of situational consciousness or national allegory – "the telling of the individual story and the individual experience cannot but ultimately involve the whole laborious telling of the collectivity itself" (*The Location of Culture,* 140).

Both Saleem Sinai and Patrick Lewis are tormented with this awareness, the too many storylines traversing their own storylines laterally. Padma, Saleem's Dung Lotus, is constantly irritated and finds herself at the end of her wits and patience as the man would not simply get down to his birth, she tells him grudgingly, "You better get a move on or you die before you get yourself born" (38). And Saleem on his part can only say that, "Things-even people – have a way of leaking into each other, like flavours when you cook. Ilse Lubin's suicide, for example, leaked into old Adam and sat there in a puddle until he saw God. Likewise the past has dripped into me ... so we can't ignore it ..." (38). Saleem cannot ignore histories, inheritances, peoples, places, love, deceits, treacheries, individual and collective optimisms and guilts that have seeped into him and his writing of the self cannot but preclude all these, he is the master of *the perforated sheet* (23) that has innumerable fissures, and each fissure has its own story waiting to be told, loosely held together by a rapidly disintegrating fabric of Saleem's failing physical and mental faculties.

While Saleem appears to be confronted with the gargantuan task of dealing with too many histories and his accidental locking of destiny with that of the nation, Patrick Lewis, on the other hand is faced with another mammoth task; it is of finding history and a past to belong to and share with. He does not have much of a personal history to hold on to or recount, he comes from one of the hinterlands of Canada and the 'whitelandscape of childhood' does not have much beside the memories of the seasonal presence besides the other the loggers who appeared seasonally like the moths and left, producing in Patrick the desire to unlock the mystery of their being. Patrick lacks the fanfare that preceded Saleem's birth, no RamRam Seth predicted his birth, no newspapers waited his birth, no prime ministers sent him framed letters with the premonitory "we will be watching you closely". Both Saleem and Patrick share a vastly different but similar dilemma, Saleem is overburdened with history and Patrick is tormented by a visible lack of history, his father taught him no mythology to hold on to, he is left to carve his own history and create his own myths. Their collective wish is to find a meaning of their life, their being, to give a purpose to it.

V.S. Naipaul in his book *India: A Wounded Civilization*, quotes a young woman who insists that "In India, I relate only to my family" (117). Naipaul is profoundly irritated by the lady's myopic sense of belonging. Naipaul's restlessness, in this context, is partially shared by Saleem and Patrick, they simply can't relate just to their families, even when they do so they find others lurking around the corner, refusing to leave, demanding an inclusion in their writings of the self. There cannot be a self without its others and no knowledge of the self is complete without the knowledge of the other. Saleem knows it and transforms himself into *All India Radio* (165); tuning into the minds of people and getting into the thick of events, while he enjoys it as a child, in his adulthood he realises that he had to do it and it was an act of self-preservation:

> "Today, with the hindsight of the lost, spent years, I can say that the spirit of self-aggrandizement which seized me then was a reflex, born of an instinct for self-preservation. If I had not believed myself in control of the flooding multitudes, their massed identities would have annihilated mine ..." (175).

Patrick on the other hand is pulled towards the other by the emptiness that surrounds him. He sees the hushed politeness of the immigrant loggers in his landscape and is enticed by their silence, as he is fascinated by the seasonal appearance of the moths:

> Perhaps he can haunt these creatures. Perhaps they are not mute at all, it is just a lack of range in his hearing. He knows the robust call from the small bodies of cicadas, but he wants conversation – the language of the damsel flies who need something to translate their breath the way he uses the ocarina to give himself a voice, something to leap with over the wall of this place. (10)

Patrick's fascination for the others speaks of a desire to know the other, to translate this silent relationship of presence in the same landscape into one which has a language. But knowing the other demands a leaping over the wall of the place and in some ways the barriers of the self.

However, it is not an easy task to transform oneself into a radio or leap over the barriers of identity, family, community. The question which arises is: are Salman Rushdie and Michael Ondaatje engaging themselves in the pure fantasy? If they are not, then what is that enables Saleem to convert himself into a radio and helps Patrick to find that language which makes communication possible between him and the others?

Homi Bhabha speaks of the creeping in of the 'unhomely moment' it's the moment when the world around the self of an individual first contracts and then expands limitlessly:

> The unhomely moment creeps upon you stealthily as your own shadow and suddenly you find yourself with Henry James's Isabel Archer, in *The Portrait of a Lady*, taking the measure of your dwelling in a state of incredulous terror. And it is at this point that the world first shrinks and then expands enormously … . In that displacement, the borders between home and world become confused; and uncannily, the private and the public become parts of each other, forcing upon us a vision that is as divided as it is disorienting. (Bhabha, 9)

Saleem's moment of the *unhomely* is his realisation of the moment when he was born with the twin nations, Nehru's letter that said his life would be a *mirror* of the nation and "We shall be watching over your life with the closest attention" (122). Patrick comes across this moment in *In the Skin of a Lion* when living among the others he discovers:

> His own life was no longer a single story but part of a mural, which was falling together of accomplices. Patrick saw a wondrous night-web – all these fragments of a human order, something ungoverned by the family he was born into or the headlines of the day. A nun on a bridge, a daredevil who was unable to sleep without a drink, a boy watching a fire from his bed at night, an actress who ran away with a millionaire – the detritus of the age was realigned. (145)

It is at this level, in their unhomed self, that Saleem and Patrick become the extended metaphors of their countries. Saleem with his immense nose and map-face carries the burden of a three thousand years old Indian civilisation, the knowledge of his true parents does not snatch his inheritance simply because he has lived it out, the knowledge reveals to him the limitations of parentage that always remains partial; he goes on to have a succession of fathers only to discover that he is the child of time fathered by history (118). Therefore, Saleem's act of writing the self throws together the tumble of public events alongside the private ones, under the persistent tick tock of the clock, Nehru and Jinnah, Amina and

Vanita, Mountbatten and Methwold, Ahmed Sinai and Wee Willie Winkie, celebrations and riots, delivery pains and burning trains, cries of the new born baby and the yells of the monster let loose in the streets and the historical speeches and silence of Adam Aziz come together and refuse to be divorced from each other. And Saleem tells an incredulous Padma "To understand just one life, you have to swallow the world" (109).

Patrick, on the other hand, feels an emptiness, "Something hollow, so when alone, when not aligned with another … . he could feel the rattle within that suggested the space between him and community. A gap of love" (157). By learning to love the other by sharing their spaces and taking responsibility, Patrick becomes a prism, becomes Canadian not because of his birth or language but by the way he aligns himself to others, feels an emptiness without them.

Both Rushdie and Ondaatje claim fathers other than their own, communities other than their own, and memories other than their own. They are against forgetting not only the memories of their own but those of the others and by refusing to forget, by inhabiting other's skins and memories they have made their works of fiction more than fiction, political statements, counter historical narratives that do not claim factual accuracy but subvert the strongest of political rhetoric and destabilise the most stable of the histories.

Midnight's Children and *In the Skin of a Lion* as the narratives of nation raise the issues of truthful representation and accountability. The governing metaphors for Rushdie in *Midnight's Children* and Ondaatje in *In the Skin of a Lion* are memory and history. These metaphors govern their narrative strategies as well as their versions of truth. Saleem does not claim authenticity because he is too aware of the corrosions and inventions that occur in the process of remembrance but nevertheless holds on to his faith in the truth of memory:

> Morality, judgment, character … it all starts with memory … . I told you the truth … Memory's truth, because memory has its own special kind. It selects, eliminates, alters, exaggerates, minimizes, glorifies, and vilifies also; but in the end it creates its

> own reality, its heterogeneous but usually coherent version of events; and no sane human being ever trusts someone else's version more than his own. (211)

Saleem admits the possibility of multiple versions, versions that may not represent the truth but are more potent than any authenticated historical truths that may present individuals and events in a breathtaking linear march but fail to cohere, providing no clues to morality, judgement, character that contain the very essence of being.

Rushdie's narrative exploits memory's fallibility to open the uncompromising seams of history, throwing a deeper light on the character and the lost flavours of history. *Midnight's Children* and *In the Skin of a Lion* as narratives of memory and history, self and nation take big leaps of imagination and invention, blending fact with fiction, material with the metaphoric, spiritual with mundane. In doing so, they problematise seriously the space of a nation as a geo-political construct. Saleem Sinai wonders about the birth of India, a myth and a nation:

> ... a new myth to celebrate, because a nation which had never previously existed was about to win its freedom, catapulting us into a world which, although it had five thousand years of history ... was nevertheless quite imaginary; into a mythical land, a country which would never exist except by the efforts of collective will – except in a dream we all dared to dream; it was a mass fantasy shared in varying degrees by Bengali and Punjabi, Madrasi and Jat, and periodically need the sanctification and renewal that which can only be provided by rituals of blood. (112)

India is as real as it is imaginary. India is a myth and a dream too but the myth and the dream of India was given a concrete shape by an act of *collective will* and collective wills are not accidental they originate from the deeper recesses of layers of civilisation and culture, relationships forged and formed through the lived reality of the complex matrix of time, space and social being.

Their constructions of self have strong political implications. They expose the official and historical lies, Rushdie exposes the tyrannies of the era of emergency and Ondaatje gives voice and life to the immigrants forgotten by the Canadian establishment. Their claims have to be juxtaposed with the claims of politics over history, the undone Saleem has to be put alongside with the claims of Indira Gandhi that no atrocities were committed during the emergency, the vanished photographs of the builders of Toronto have to be put alongside the grand snaps of the planners and the architects of the city. Rushdie's and Ondaatje's fiction does it in multiple ways. Graham Greene attacking a journalist remarked, "A petty reason perhaps why novelists more and more try to keep a distance from journalists is that novelists are trying to write the truth and journalists are trying to write fiction" (217). To this the politicians may be added because in the contemporary world they have become the master weavers of fiction and with all their freedom now have to carry the additional responsibility of telling the truth, exposing the political fictions.

Amnesia is the worst curse that a nation can be infected with. Loss of memory is the loss the self and the self of the nation. Jose Arcadio Buendia in *One Hundred Years of Solitude* frantically attempts to save the inhabitants of Macondo from the spell of amnesia, that began with insomnia and led to the erasure of childhood memories, "then the name and notion of things, and finally the identity of people and even the awareness of his own being, until he sank into a kind of idiocy that had no past" (45). The loss of memory succumbs the people of Macondo 'to the spell of an imaginary reality, one invented by themselves' (49) and to the mystifications of Pilar Ternera who started 'reading their past as she had read the future before' (49). Loss of memory makes the people create imaginary realities and live in them. It reduces them to a vulnerable mass that can be moulded at will by *mystifications* of their past by politicians and fortune-tellers alike.

Ondaatje and Rushdie are against forgetting not only the memories of their own but those of the others and by refusing to forget, by inhabiting others' skins and memories they have made their works of fiction more than fiction, political statements, counter historical narratives that do not claim factual accuracy but subvert the strongest of political rhetoric and destabilise the most stable of the histories. Edward Said, voicing the Palestinian cause, brings out the pain of a homeland that survives only in the mind, remarks, "The interesting thing is that there seems to be nothing in the world which sustains the story: unless you go on telling it, it will just drop and disappear" (*Imaginary Homelands*, 178).

The act of not allowing the memory to disappear and keeping it alive by a perpetual telling has kept Palestine alive. So does Rushdie consider the 'feasibility of the chutnification of history; the grand hope of the pickling of time!' (459). Though the process admits the possibility of distortions but it has the power to preserve the flavours of history and memory 'changed in degree not in kind' (461). While Saleem Sinai's jars of pickled histories and memories wait to be 'unleashed upon the amnesiac nation,' he emphasises the need of constant revisions, 'The process of revision should be constant and endless; don't think that I'm satisfied with what I've done!' He leaves one jar empty (462).

Nation, even without a slight change in its geographical boundaries, is in a state of perpetual transformation, making and unmaking. It is as imaginary as it is real and it requires consistent *sanctification and renewal*, which does not always have to *be provided by rituals of blood*, insofar our imagination transcends the barriers of castes, class, religion and language and drive its life force from the socially produced spaces, lived and shared experiences that bind the self with the other, with our environs our histories and memories. The narratives of history and memory like *Midnight's Children* and *In the Skin of a Lion* play a crucial role in this context. They are, in a way, the rituals of sanctification and renewal that the nation requires.

Through their journeys into the private and the collective pasts, digressions and inventions they put the imaginary homelands in a realistic perspective and on firmer grounds. Their assumption of the nation in narration juxtaposes the historical truth with the truth of experience, linearity of events with extensions into the horizontal lived and living spaces across the barriers of temporality. In this process they offer a strong resistance to mystifications, political or otherwise, of collective histories and memories and open the space of a nation in its continual state of revisions and reformulations. Each of these narratives reinvents the nation in its own way and its return to past is firmly grounded in the desire to give meaning to the present. And though memory, at one level, is a mourning, in these narratives it is not a mourning without possibilities.

A bridge goes up in *In the Skin of a Lion* and a world and its art crumble in *The English Patient*. Ondaatje's creation of the counter-sites of construction and destruction in the two novels is structurally and thematically metaphoric in nature. There is simultaneous construction and deconstruction. Ondaatje juxtaposes the official makers (the city-planners and architects) and the real makers (the immigrant workers) of the bridge and deconstructs the official history. There are other bridges in the making-in-between the immigrant communities and a possible bridge between the domineering centre and its periphery.

Patrick Lewis in the climactic scene in *In the Skin of a Lion* turns away from destroying the water-filtration plant. Ondaatje circumvents the fictional possibilities of the destruction of the water-plant by Patrick or Patrick's arrest by the officials that in either case would have been a strong statement of the immigrants' reaction to the establishmentarian coldness. The novel ends with a dialogue between Commissioner Harris and Patrick. Commissioner Harris is forced to shrug off the official *defensive* demeanour and to meet the real makers of the country half way on the bridge Patrick seeks to build.

Ondaatje emphasises the opening of a dialogic space between the centre and its periphery and the subversiveness of the immigrant communities does not seek destruction but an acknowledgement, respect and space, an intimacy in the country they have come to be. Similarly, in *The English Patient*, as the world collapses at the hands of its politicians, there are regenerative forces that seek to build new bridges of human relationships beyond the constraints of cultures, nation-states and identities. Almásy dies, Hana, Caravaggio and Kirpal Singh return to their countries but the experience of togetherness, the curing of the self by curing the other, has transformed them for ever. They meet in a liminal space and depart but the distances between them are immaterial insofar as they remember that bridges exist and can always be constructed between the farthest of the geographical spaces, between the past and the present, between cultures and the colours of skins. All it takes is an effort and the belief like Queen Sheba's in the *sacredness* of the bridges.

Ondaatje's politics has evolved with his poetics and this evolution has a visible manifestation in his novel *Anil's Ghost*. With *Anil's Ghost* Ondaatje turns back to Sri Lanka after eighteen years of the publication of his family memóir *Running in the Family*. Both the books share an interesting relationship as they represent the evolving nature of the expatriate sensibility and the sense of belonging. The expatriate writers in their treatment of adopted and inherited spaces concentrate primarily on issues that deal with their coming to terms with the new culture, the trauma of dislocation and a search for identity and roots in their past. They often show a nostalgic clinging to the homes they knew.

Ondaatje's *Running in the Family* is also partially nostalgic; Ondaatje's persistent concern in the book is pre-independence Ceylon rather than contemporary Sri Lanka. *Anil's Ghost* picks up what was left out in *Running in the Family*, the massive bloodshed and the politics of ethnic violence and the counter strategies of the Government in contemporary Sri Lanka. The shocking upsurge of ethnic violence and the rise of fundamentalism in the last few decades in South Asia, is strong enough to jolt any complacent indulgence in nostalgia and standard depictions of the first spaces of belonging. It brings into stark contrast the relatively *safer* trauma of being in an alien landscape and the magnitude of the sufferings of the people back home who did not and do not have the choices of escape.

The search for roots and identity cannot remain untouched by the chaos of the present, as the threads to both lie buried in the past of the country. The crisis in the countries of origin puts the expatriates in a complex position of contradictory impulses and allegiances. Can he or she disown the present of the countries of their origin? Can they assume a neutral position or identify themselves with the so-called *humanistic* stance of the West towards their country? If not, what position should they take? Can they still commit themselves to a cause despite the distance and western citizenships?

Michael Ondaatje's *Anil's Ghost* reveals a characteristic concern with the contemporary ethnic clashes in his country of origin Sri – Lanka. During the last few decades, Sri Lanka has experienced one of the worst and the most prolonged civil wars in human history. In fact a majority of countries in South Asia – India, Pakistan, Nepal, Bhutan, Mynamar, Indonesia and the Philippines – are in the grip of ethnic violence, religious fundamentalism, narrow definitions of castes and creeds and the corresponding demands for separate regions and self-governance. In Sri Lanka there has been a demand for a separate *Tamil Eelem* by the Tamils the largest minority group in the country. The clash has resulted in thousands of deaths, never ending terror and the existence of a nation within a nation with understood but officially unacknowledged boundaries:

> It was a Hundred Year's War with modern weaponry, and backers on the sidelines in safe countries, a war sponsored by gun- and drug-runners. It became evident that political enemies were secretly joined in financial arms deals. *'The reason for war was war'*. (43)

The democratic set-ups in South Asia have not proved effective in handling the crisis. Governments with professed secular intentions, constitutions, countless laws and sub-laws that promise civil liberty regardless of race, caste, class, gender and religion have failed to come to terms with the upsurge of ethnic violence and very often they turn out to be more lethal and destructive than the terrorist factions in these countries. In the recent past Asia has emerged as the biggest victim of government-sponsored disappearances.[1]

Anil, a forensic scientist, comes to Sri Lanka to investigate 'disappearances' and their possible connection with the government. Anil, like Ondaatje, left Sri Lanka when the seeds of ethnic hatred were yet to erupt. She returns after fifteen years, to find herself in a strange place caught up in blood bath and *the national disease of fear* (53). Her parents are dead and she only has a few scattered relatives on the land. The family pulls are minimised by Ondaatje. Anil's dedication to her profession, the absence of an immediate family, and her present task puts her in an apparently neutral position in relation to the island:

> The island no longer held her by the past. She'd spent fifteen years since ignoring that early celebrity. Anil had read documents and news reports, full of tragedy, and she had now lived abroad long enough to interpret Sri Lanka with a long-distance gaze. But here it was a more complicated world morally. The streets were still streets, the citizens remained citizens. They shopped, changed jobs, laughed. Yet the darkest Greek tragedies were innocent compared with what was happening here. (11)

Anil's is the expatriate's predicament. There are no easy solutions or judgements to be passed but at the same time the graveness of the situation disrupts the possibility of a poised neutral stance. The long years abroad and the gradual wearing out of the family links and emotional strings do provide the expatriate with the long distance gaze but a stepping back into the former homes brings back multiple pulls, sensations that the body seems to have grown unaccustomed to, in the new landscapes of adopted homes. It is a physical response, in the West Anil had read about Asia that there *The dawn comes up like thunder* (9) and she was the only one to recognise the phrase physically. The weather, streets, people, famous shops, saloons, fans, they all come back, in a way, breaking the barriers of time spent away from home.

The expatriate sensibility operates in multiple temporal and spatial frames. There is both the conscious and unconscious remembering, every object seen forces associations for different reasons – for being the same, for being changed, for being forgotten, for being new. There is an unconscious mapping of the home space and as it merges and departs from the remembered, heard or imagined mappings of the home with and through the distance of time and space. Also there are frequent and consistent interventions from the adopted homes, the acquired, evolved and forced sensibilities, the translatability of time into international times. While Anil feels her past on the island coming to life with clear imprints in the familiar surroundings of Sri Lankan landscape, there is the consistent need to remain in touch with adopted home in the West. Even a picture postcard from her friend Leaf comes as a great source of relief (29). With these, there is the consciousness of being viewed as partially a foreigner, being a celebrity for some, a prodigal for others, the slight distancing or discreet treatment of the people at home. While these impulses, sensations and different levels of consciousness exercise their intricate pulls there is the urge to come to terms with the chaotic present of the home country both as a citizen and as a human being.

In *Anil's Ghost,* Ondaatje searches meaning, understanding and, in a way, resolution of the contemporary crisis, in history and archaeology of the island. Archaeology becomes the governing metaphor and the organisational principle in the book. The earth is a vast reservoir of the layers of civilisations, the sublime chronicle that captures the temporality of all times into the timeless:

> The most precisely recorded moments of history lay adjacent to the extreme actions of nature or civilization. She knew that. Pompeii. Laetoli. Hiroshima. Vesuvius (whose fumes had asphyxiated poor Pliny while he recorded its 'tumultuous behaviour'). Tectonic slips and brutal human violence provided random time-capsules of unhistorical lives. A dog in Pompeii. A gardener's shadow in Hiroshima. But in the midst of such events, she realized there could never be any logic to the human violence without the distance of time. (55)

Ondaatje puts together history, archaeology, forensics, surgery, politics, the acts of violence and threads of belonging in a complex organic relationship. He works through juxtapositions and overlapping of one into the other. Anil is teamed up with Sarath who considers the pairing of a forensic anthropologist with an archaeologist odd (17). But the organised acts of violence in the contemporary world tie archaeology and forensics in a strange relationship. People are kidnapped, killed, burnt and buried to hide evidence converting the earth into a vast graveyard with layers of civilisation and evidence of contemporary crimes put together at random. While Anil deals with deliberate burials and erasures of evidence, Sarath deals with the burials and erasures that have occurred with the passage of time.

The strange association of archaeology with forensics has its own ironical implications. The random acts of burials by nature or humans disturb the synchronicity of ages and blur the clear lines of distinction between the historical and the contemporary. Every act of violence has its precedent – the skeleton named 'Sailor' by Anil is an evidence of a contemporary act of violence but the other decapitated skeletons of the sixth century Buddhist monks 'Tinker', 'Tailor', and 'Soldier' have also probably been the victims of violence (51).

The chaos of the present, its violence, the splits in the self and the negotiation of multiple belongings has its roots in history and meaning, missing links gradually unfold as the layers of a buried past are gradually revealed with the tender brush strokes of an archaeologist. There is the translatability of one time into others and one space into other spaces. Anil concentrates on a search, it is the search for the body, face and a name of an anachronous skeleton but in her mind she is aware that it is not a crime limited to Sri Lanka. She has worked in different spaces, Guatemala, Congo and is aware there are other places wounded by similar crimes, other places being converted into vast burial grounds. And there is the awareness that while she and Sarath burrow into the past to establish the identity of Sailor, the landscape around them receives newer bodies. Every step forward is a move backwards into time and space. An archeologist, a historian, a searcher has to work with this sense of irony around him or her:

> There are images carved into or painted on rock – a perspective of a village seen from the height of a nearby hill, a single line depicting a woman's back bent over a child – that have altered Sarath's perceptions of his world ... . These were discoveries made during the worst political times, alongside a thousand dirty little acts of race and politics, gang madness and financial gain. War having come this far like a poison into the bloodstream could not get out ... . Half the world, it felt, was being buried, the truth hidden by fear, while the past revealed itself in the light of a burning rhododendron bush. (156)

The search for a lost identity recurs in Ondaatje. In *The Collected Works of Billy the Kid* (1970) the search is for the self of a legendary outlaw William Bonney; in *Coming Through Slaughter* (1976) the search is for an obscure Black jazz cornetist Buddy Bolden; in the memóir *Running in the Family* (1982) it is the search for a lost father and family ties; in *In the Skin of a Lion* Patrick searches for a lost millionaire Ambrose Small; in *The English Patient,* there is the burnt, faceless English patient whose identity is shrouded in the dark. None of the searches is conclusive, even when the identities are revealed they are in the momentary flashes of recognition, a deliberate disruption of the boundaries between the subject, the author and the reader. In *Anil's Ghost* the search does not end with the establishment of Sailor's identity.

The inherent irony of history and archaeology, the extension of the past into present and the intervention of present into past problematises the nature of truth. While Anil from her experience in the West has come to expect clearly marked roads to every discovery and holds truth above everything else (44); there are others, Sarath, Gamini, Palipana and Ananda, who hold on to different perceptions of truth. Sarath knows that truth is important but is dangerous in a time of crisis:

> It was a flame against a sleeping lake of petrol. Sarath had seen truth broken into suitable pieces and used by foreign press alongside irrelevant photographs. A flippant gesture towards Asia that might lead, as a result of this information, to new vengeance and slaughter. There were dangers in handing truth to an unsafe city around you. As an archaeologist Sarath believed in truth as a principle. That is, he would give his life for truth if truth was of any use. (156–157)

For Gamini the only truth that is important is to patch up the victims of violence, until the newer bodies arrived. For Palipana truth lies in the submerged histories, banned stories, unwritten epigraphs and lost links of civilisation. For Ananda there is no truth but the calm and serenity he wishes to see on the face of his lost wife and recreates it in the face of 'Sailor' (184). For Sri Lanka truth is too obvious to be proved and much more important is the holding on to hope. And with these there is the Western version of truth and its prerogative of authenticating truth.

Anil's Ghost calls into question the role of the West, its self-assumed authority of being the sole judicator and representative of human rights while it simultaneously houses the terrorist headquarters and the human rights offices, supplies the weapons of destruction to governments and terrorists without any discrimination, makes and breaks dictators and sends in international referees or armies to ensure peace and harmony. Anil's arrival in Sri Lanka is also the result of such a *gesture* by the West and though she has a very specific task to perform nobody at the human rights office had much of a hope about the success of the mission (16). Anil's past experience has taught her:

> The grand logos on letterheads and European office doors meant nothing where there was crisis. If and when you were asked by a government to leave, you left. You took nothing with you. Not a slide tray, not a piece of film. At the airport, while they searched her clothing, she'd sat almost naked on a stool. (29)

The apparent impotence of Western authority partially speaks of the nexus between the West, the terrorist organisations and governments eager to maintain supremacy. Countries struggling with poverty, hunger and unemployment have emerged as potential markets for arms manufacturers from the West in the post-cold war era. War has to be kept alive for economic and political reasons which otherwise may prove a threat to flourishing arms industry and the authority of the West. The so-called humanitarian concern of the West is diplomatically tempered, that ensures that the problems are not completely resolved, keeping the doors open for a constant presence and future interventions.

The West has used Human Rights as a double-edged weapon. It becomes the pretext for the Western intervention into the autonomy of the Third World countries. An Afghanistan or an Iraq can be routed for the possible presence of the weapons of mass destruction that ironically have their largest storehouses in the West. The complacence of the Western attitude towards these countries finds a projection in Western movies:

> The American or the Englishman gets on a plane and leaves. That's it. The camera leaves with him. He looks out of the window at Mombassa or Vietnam or Jakarta, someplace now he can look at through the clouds. The tired Hero. A couple of words to the girl beside him. He is going. So the war, to all practical purposes, is over. That's enough reality for the West. (286)

The truth of politics and the truth of humanity are juxtaposed in the novel and with power being on its side the truth of politics appears to get the better of it. The fate of millions hangs in abyss as the West, terrorist factions and the governments wrestle for power or join hands secretly to remain in the centre. Though history and archaeology with the distance of time may provide some meaning to the prevailing violence in the acknowledgement that human civilisation has never been without it; but even then, the stark visibility, the physical presence of violence and its victims challenge a passive acceptance and demand resolution in the present.

Anil's Ghost is a novel dedicated to the professionals who despite all the madness around them are engaged in countering the forces of destruction with an obsessive reconstruction. Anil, Sarath, Gamini, Palipana, Ananda are people who love their professions and cling to them with a single-minded devotion. Though they all have suffered personal anguish, Anil's parents died in an accident, Sarath's wife committed suicide, Gamini's marriage failed, Palipana's brother, a monk, was brutally murdered and Ananda's wife became a victim of abduction. But they emerge from their personal sorrows to play a part in the healing of their wounded nation. It is a kind of positive escape from personal sorrows. Anil gets obsessed with a single skeleton she has the faith that: *One village can speak for many villages. One victim can speak for many victims* (176).

Sarath, Palipana, Gamini and Ananda with all their awareness of the dangers of truth come together with Anil in her mission. Sarath loses his life in the process but not before seeing Anil safely through, along with her finds and proofs to establish the truth. Palipana the epigraphist, who has retreated from the world to the Grove of the Ascetics plays his part by directing Anil and Sarath to Ananda. Ananda the artist who specialised in painting of the eyes of Buddha and became a gem-pit miner after the death of his wife comes out of his pain and reconstructs the skull of the Sailor that leads to his identification. And in the last section of the book he directs a large team of artists to reconstruct the statue of Buddha (306).

Their coming together is a coincidence ironically made possible by the prevailing violence. Among the most tender of Anil's discoveries has been:

> ... the tracks at Laetoli – almost-four-million-year-old footsteps of a pig, a hyena, a rhinoceros and a bird, this strange ensemble identified by a twentieth-century tracker. Four unrelated creature that had walked hurriedly over a wet layer of volcanic ash. To get away from what? ... It was that quartet of animals walking from Laetoli four million years ago that she liked to think about. (55)

There are situations and images that recur in Ondaatje, while the quartet of four unrelated humans appeared in *The English Patient* – Almásy, Hana, Cravaggio and Kirpal Singh, it reappears in *Anil's Ghost* – Anil, Sarath, Gamini and Ananda. The quartet was brought together by the Second World War in *The English Patient* in *Anil's Ghost* it is brought together by the contemporary civil war in Sri Lanka. There is the image of the burnt faceless English patient and Hana's obsessive attachment with him, in *Anil's Ghost* there is Anil and the skeleton and then Palipana rapidly going blind with a young girl in the Grove of the Ascetics (84). Obsession operates at the centre of these novels, individuals hold on to each other and in complex ways heal each other. Perhaps the only way to maintain sanity in the times of crisis is to engage in a communal healing.

The novel ends on a note of hope, with a vision. Though Anil leaves the island eventually this departure is different from that of the disinterested Western hero. She carries the ghosts of Sarath and the thousands of others and their muffled cries. The voices will never leave her and she is determined not to let these ghosts die. She wants the entire world to see them amid all its politics and *three-dimensional chess moves and back-room deals* (28) of diplomacy and international relations. Ananda directs the reconstruction of a huge statue of Buddha and performs the ceremony of *Netra Mangala*, painting the eyes of god, the eyes that make the statue, a god. For few brief moments Ananda shares the vision of god. The difference of ages getting blurred in the surrounding darkness and from the distance every *fibre of human history* (307) and existence is made visible.

Note

1. Political hostiles, primarily from the minorities, are taken into custody without judicial warrants, there is no documentation and the victims simply vanish. It is not to suggest that only governments are responsible for the atrocities and disappearances but the shocking part is that the governments in South Asia appear to have adopted abductions as a tactical device to eliminate opposition. The numbers are astounding, according to Amnesty International figures – more than 40,000 in Sri

Lanka since 1988, 4,000 in Kashmir since 1989, 1,600 in Philippines since 1970.

Works Cited

Bhabha, Homi. *The Location of Culture*. London: Routledge, 1994.

Heble, Ajay. ""Rumours of Topography": The Cultural Politics of Michael Ondaatje's *Running in the Family*." *Essays on Canadian Writing*. No. 53, 186–203 (Summer, 1994).

Huggan, Graham. "Exoticism and Ethnicity in Michael Ondaatje's *Running in the Family*." *Essays on Canadian Writing*. No. 57, 116–27, Winter 1995.

Mukherjee, Arun. "The Poetry of Michael Ondaatje and Cyril Dabydeen: Two Responses to Otherness." *Journal of Canadian Literature*. 20, No. I, 49–67 (Spring, 1985).

Ondaatje, Michael. *Anil's Ghost* (2000). New Delhi: Picador India, 2000.

——. *The English Patient* (1992). Toronto: Vintage Books, 1993.

——. *In the Skin of a Lion*. Toronto: McClelland and Stewart, 1987.

——. *Running in the Family*. Toronto: McClelland, 1982.

——. *Coming Through Slaughter* (1976). Toronto: Picador, 1984.

——. *Collected Works of Billy the Kid: Left Handed Poems* (1970). Toronto: Picador,1989.

Sugunari, Suwanda H.J. "'Sri Lankan' Canadian Poets: The Bourgeoise That Fled the Revolution." *Canadian Literature*. 132, 60–79 (1992).

6

The Poetics of Exile

You tell me to pack up my bags and go
But where? I turn my face towards
Country after country
Silently I lip read their refusal
What do I call myself?
Exile, émigré refugee

Jean Arasanayagam, *Exile II*

So many years to learn
We are not sinful people
And passion is everywhere appropriate

Suniti Namjoshi, *Because of India*[1]

The poetics of exile, the literature of the diasporas, has come a long way from the *curse* of aphasia to a speaking out, from a loss of the filial ties to a retributive order of belonging, from nostalgia to amnesia to a conscious remembering, from the 'then and there' to the 'now and here' and 'beyond'. The path has never been linear nor the experiences unilateral. The inherent diversity of the poetics of exile has endowed it with much of its vigour and character though it is difficult to devise standard critical parameters to fathom the multiplicities of the poetics of exile. Dislocation in all its complex implications may serve as a benchmark, a useful point of departure towards an understanding of the poetics of exile.

The visible *constants* in poetics of exile – dislocation, trauma, private and public histories, identity, culture and allegiances – are ironically the *variables* that are manifested in complexly intricate patterns in the subjective self of the exiles, diasporas, refugees and immigrants and their creative expressions. These denominators have an inherent paradox, they can both be instruments of entrapment and of release. A majority of the literature of the diasporas harbours this paradox and it underlies the distinctiveness within the poetics of exile.

Writers like V.S. Naipaul, Salman Rushdie, Ashish Gupta, Rohinton Mistry, M.J. Vassanji, Neil Bissoondath and Bharati Mukherjee have responded to this paradox in their own characteristic manners, from different positions and perspectives. The commonality of their South Asian descent can hardly account for the distinctiveness of their aesthetics and creative expressions. The trauma of being one of *Midnight's Children* can hardly find a reflection in the trauma of being a plantation labourer in the Caribbean, holding fast to an idyllic notion of homeland and the shattering discovery of *An Area of Darkness*. The marginality of Parsi community in India and the Burghers in Sri Lanka speaks of different experiences. These writers inherit diverse cultural backgrounds and have come across distinctive experiences evolving individualistic sensibilities and ways to relate to the worlds within and outside.

Ondaatje's poetics brings to surface the inherent versatility of the poetics of exile. He has not engaged himself in standardised response to his otherness. His creation of the myth of Billy the Kid reveals his initial efforts to discover a voice through an assumption of a western historical/legendary figure. He creates a subtly convincing picture of the outlaw thoroughly integrated in his violence, who consistently remains on the periphery. Ondaatje took up another peripheral character in *Coming Through Slaughter* and after inhabiting the skins of the cultural others Ondaatje turned to gauge his belonging to Sri Lanka and Canada with *Running in the Family* and *In the Skin of a Lion*.

Ondaatje does not negotiate his belonging in terms of stereotypical renditions of nostalgia and the pains of marginalisation, he brings together various perspectives and attempts to comprehend Sri Lanka and Canada beyond his own subjective position and relationships with these countries. By putting together others' threads of belonging alongside his own, he attempts to situate the web of relationships (cultural, ethnic, and national) in broader context. Ondaatje's treatment of time and space and his narrative and structural strategies reveal different times and spaces in their simultaneous similarities and distances. Ondaatje's political perspective has gradually evolved. The initial evasiveness has given way to his delving into the larger and more public issues. But here again Ondaatje avoids being caught up in the narrow political allegiances or approaches. His concerns remain broadly humanitarian.

Journeys serve as a universal symbol in the poetics of exile. There are journeys across geographies and cultures, from one mode of being to another, from the physical to the subjective, from the material to the metaphoric, and from the private to the public. None of these journeys can be seen exclusively in terms of points of origins and destinations, they signify a to and fro movement where the points of origin become destinations and the destinations become points of departure. Neil Bissoondath underlines the crucial significance of the journey to one's land of origin, "For many the journey is inevitable: establishing oneself in a new land is always difficult; the effort can make the land left behind seem idyllic, and often only renewed contact will evoke the reasons for initial departure and at last cast the new land and the life it offers in a sharper, more compelling light. It is a sentimental journey that many, and even most immigrants must make before they can truly move on with their lives" (Bissoondath, 126). For many the journey can be a shattering experience. V.S. Naipaul underwent a similar shocking realisation during his first visit to India, "It was a journey that ought not to have been made; it had broken my life in two" (qtd. by Bissoondath, 131).

In Ondaatje's case the journey produces a contradictory result, it helps him to negotiate the split in his self. Ondaatje's poetics does not speak of a settled state or perspective, but it has evolved beyond his journey from Sri Lanka to England and from England to Canada. His works of fiction are structured as journeys: *The Collected Works of Billy the Kid* presents the journey of an outlaw into a legend and into a myth. *Coming Through Slaughter* is the journey of an artist to that perfect edge where the barriers between the art and its creator fall and the form becomes the content. *Running in the Family* is Ondaatje's journey into the Ceylon of his parents' generation. *In the Skin of a Lion* is structured as a journey, and brings together multiple journeys – the journeys of the East European immigrants to Canada, Patrick's journey from the white landscape of his childhood to the metropolis, his journey from a searcher of Ambrose Small to the mythical journey of Gilgamesh. *The English Patient* is a reservoir of journeys across time and spaces, revealing the constraints of fixed identities and their vulnerabilities, journey from a sense of loss in the self to a compensation in love for the other. *Anil's Ghost* is an expatriate's journey into the landscape of origin beyond the personal relationships and nostalgia to seek a newer belonging and responsibility, the journey from countering violence to the *eyes* of Buddha, an unfailing faith in redemption and an understanding.

Aritha Van Herk considers the problem of the universal and the particular in the context of the poetics of exile. She points out the power of the 'overt story' to obfuscate the 'covert story' and the necessity of articulating the 'overlooked obvious story', the 'secret' and the 'absent stories', "These stories are the same but differently tainted: oxymorons of themselves, a contradictory reflectance. They offer every writer a Parisian choice. No matter which goddess he favoured, Paris would have purchased disaster, but his choice has dictated the story ... and problematizing covert story, is the true crisis of every writer who wishes to entext the immigrant experience" (Van Herk, 177–178). Even if the choice is Parisian, it is there. This choice finds a visible reflection the expatriate writer's treatment of history.

A recourse to history is almost inevitable in the experience of dislocation as it provides the dislocated a sense of belonging and security from the fear of anonymity. But an impulsive historicising of one's ethnicity may lead to an entrapment in an illusion. Neil Bissoondath brings out the nature of this illusion, "To see oneself in history rather than outside it, to see oneself as a victim of history rather than as one of its victimizers, is to confer oneself a delicious sweet-and-sour confirmation of one's existence: deliciously sweet because you cannot be denied; deliciously sour because you have been brutalized. This life you lead is not your fault" (Bissoondath, 103). Such a view of history is self defeating, a perverse engagement with masochism. Similarly a narrow alliance with communal histories to discover 'identity' proves equally misleading, identity is not an object to unearthed from the silt of history but it has to cultivated and negotiated through the layers of histories.

Engagement with history is a potential tool of empowerment in the poetics of exile. However, the nature of this empowerment is highly problematic and its roots can be traced precisely in the domain and the discourse through which this empowerment is sought. The writers very often choose to engage in racial communal histories, histories of the "homeland" and even in the context of the adopted homes, concentrate on the experiences of their *own* communities. It can be granted that what is self-experienced and best known can be best expressed but such expressions may not be necessarily empowering as they may further authenticate the exile's estrangement, his/her marginality in the power structures.

Voicing the silenced, marginalised, ignored histories from narrow communal perspectives carries its own paradox, foregrounding one history is an overlooking of other histories equally marginalised and ignored. Margins writing, addressing colonial/postcolonial centres stigmatising them for their deliberate obliteration and ignorance while themselves ignoring their immediate *disenfranchised* neighbours. It is locking one's being and fate in an inheritance of marginality that refuses to leave and it facilitates the official divisiveness where the individual is always *less than or equal to* his culture of origin, a redundant stereotype.

More importantly, the consistent operation within narrow communal/cultural confines is a denial of the history of the country in which the exile has come to be. This history too demands an endearment like the communal/cultural histories, keeping oneself out of it and relating to it only in a narrow cultural/communal perspective is double treason, to the citizenship, to the immigrant cause, to the community and to the self. History is always in the making, and to find a place in history as a product of historical lamentations can hardly be fulfilling.

Ondaatje has negotiated histories, private and public, communal, national in multiple ways. He does not approach these histories from a settled perspective or singular positions. His engagement with history speaks of a constant search for belonging beyond the obvious claims of race, community or geo-political boundaries. *Running in the Family* though partially nostalgic is not a mourning, a romance with a disappeared past. With all his love for his family, relatives and the landscape of his childhood, Ondaatje both runs in and runs out of his family and searches for a newer belonging. He contextualises the perspectives of the colonisers, the adventure seekers, his own hybrid community and that of the natives with each other and the island. He sees the absences, historical and contemporary, within these relationships and grasping them, seeks to construct his own belonging.

In his treatment of the adopted home Canada in *In the Skin of a Lion*, Ondaatje does not speak from his own subject position as a Third World immigrant or a South Asian Canadian nor does he create a contemporary situation. By taking up the stories of the other (White) immigrants Ondaatje relates to the challenges of the immigrant in a broader way, going beyond his own community. Ondaatje establishes affiliative ties with the immigrant communities and Canada. By moving into the establishmentarian history of Canada and forging an ex-centric, unofficial history of the making of the nation, Ondaatje stakes a bigger claim over Canada than might not be possible speaking from a narrow communal perspective. This sense of community and compensatory relationships is taken further in *The English Patient*. Almásy, Hana, Kip and Caravaggio discover relationships and belonging beyond the borders of nationalistic claims over identity.

Nino Ricci points out, "Many immigrants hold on to romantic visions of their country which has changed dramatically since they left, and this contributes to a distortion of their identity. In their own country, they would have evolved with the customs of that country. And here, they hold strong to this idealized traditional notion of their culture." The tendency accounts partially for the reluctance of the immigrants to come to terms with the transformed present of their countries of origin. Ondaatje's *Anil's Ghost* is a far cry from the narratives of nostalgia. The extremely focused effort in *Anil's Ghost* emphasises an assumption of responsibility beyond the *sweet-sour* memories and the *ghosts* of an irretrievable past. Ondaatje's own community chose to remain out of the ethnic conflict and its politics and a majority of them sought newer destinations in western countries, deserting their own nativity and responsibility in favour of the genealogical affiliation with Europe.

Ondaatje's deliberate engagement with the Sri Lankan politics in the present acquires an interesting relationship with the other deliberate assumptions of political responsibilities by other immigrants from South Asia. The politics of exile, to a great extent, takes its texture from the concerns with ethnic and commercial interests in the "homeland". A majority of separatist movements in the South Asia are propelled and sustained by 'international funding' coming from the immigrants who have come to believe in 'ethnic homelands.' The tracks of the funds for the struggles for a Khalistan, Bodoland and Kashmir in India and *Tamil Eelam* in Sri Lanka are too visible to be missed out. Then there are upbeat expatriate global businessmen ready to pounce upon any commercial opportunity to *invest* in the countries of origin, receiving laurels for their interest and making big money in the process. Ondaatje's *Anil's Ghost* offers a nice contrast to such pseudo patriotisms. The initial tentativeness of belonging in *Running in the Family* is taken over by definite sense of responsibility towards the country that claims a physical involvement in the present; the wounds cannot be nursed by an aversion into a subjective nostalgic haze or by picking up narrow economic or 'ethnic' causes.

Appropriation of myths and myth making plays a crucial role in the expatriate experience. Ondaatje has appropriated established myths, has broken and rearranged and restructured them in his works. Mythical mode has allowed Ondaatje to go beyond the socio-cultural specifics of the spaces of his origin and of adoption and to relate to the larger structures and recurring patterns of human faith and aspirations. Ondaatje has used myths in multiple ways to counter tyrannical historical determinations, to situate the personal into the broader frameworks, to question the constraints of identity, to explore the relationships between the self and the other, the otherness of the self and the selfhood of the other and to negotiate existence.

His mythical approach has evolved from the appropriation of the cowboy legend in *The Collected Works of Billy the Kid* to the pietas in *Anil's Ghost*. The appropriation of the myth of Billy the Kid was Ondaatje's entry into the western psyche and it partially speaks of his own cultural appropriation by western myths as a subject of colonial Ceylon. Ondaatje transforms the legend of Billy the Kid into a myth and establishes interesting parallels between the outlaw/artist/outsider. He brings into consideration the processes of identity determinations and exposes them in their vulnerabilities. Similarly the figure of Buddy Bolden, the unrecorded New Orleans musician, offers Ondaatje to inhabit the skin of the other and, through his beautiful but dangerously self-annihilating immersion into his art, allows Ondaatje to negotiate his own relationship with art.

In *Running in the Family* Ondaatje explores the mythical formulations of his island home Ceylon that enticed the entire Europe. He also indulges in the folk myths prevalent on the island and creates his private myths – the myth of an eccentric father and an entire dissipating generation. With *In the Skin of a Lion* he appropriates the Babylonian myth of Gilgamesh and converts it into a contemporary myth of resistance between the centre and the periphery whereby the settled positions are brought off hinges and there is a transference of roles, responsibilities and a sharing; an emphasis on the building of bridges between the binaries, the polar opposites and the negotiation of a more human order. *The English Patient* has multiple mythical underpinnings. Almásy is alternately seen as Odysseus, the Knight of Ravenna, David, the Egyptian traveller and the others like Kirpal Singh as *Kim,* the warrior saint, and Hana as *Abhishag*, the *Queen of Sheba* and Caravaggio too has a counterpart in the painter Caravaggio. *Anil's Ghost* has the myth of mourning, a sense of loss, the faith to replace trauma with a possible serenity, a craving for the vision of God in simultaneous intimacy and distance.

Ondaatje's narrative, structural strategies have finessed from one work to another. His poetic ambition of 'harnessing images with words' or to touch frozen operas of the past into words has found a concrete realisation in his later works. From *The Collected Works of Billy the Kid*, the potpourri of literary genres, photographs, newspaper clippings and comic book legends, Ondaatje's narrative structural strategies have evolved as he has moved from poetry to writing (poetic) fiction.

The experimental approach of Billy the Kid required Ondaatje to use visual images and photographs to fill up the gaps, to give direction to the narrative, to restrain or to extend it. But gradually Ondaatje has replaced the visual images with strongly visual verbal images. His novels can be read as extended images or poems in prose. *Billy the Kid* and *Coming Through Slaughter* present a poet's movement into prose, the fragmented narrative, sudden digressions of these works acquire a subtlety in the later works. The fragmentations, digressions and regressions are harmonised into the structures of *In the Skin of a Lion, The English Patient* and *Anil's Ghost*. All the works of Ondaatje foreground a search but none of the narratives unfold in a linear, sequential manner. He has incorporated the non-literary genres of history and documentary into his technique and through his fictional renderings has tested the limits of the settled modes of representation.

In Ondaatje's hands history reads like fiction and his fiction appears more 'historical' than history. He has successfully negotiated what Ajay Heble calls 'the problem of history' with a consistent juxtaposition of history alongside myth, biography, the silences within history and through constant blurring of the borders between them. The self-reflexivity of the different modes and that of Ondaatje's own text tantalises 'fixed' perspectives but proves a wholesome experience, a startling realisation of the missing links, a sudden emergence of order.

Such moments constantly recur in Ondaatje's texts. Almásy discovers such a moment in the desert where identity loses its significance; Hana finds such a moment nursing the ceaseless wounds of the victims of war when bodies around her melt into one large human body; and Kip sees his brother and himself in the murals on the ceilings of Italian churches; Caravaggio sees the meaning in Hana aligning herself to an unknown burnt man. Anil sees a woman who had lost her husband and a son placing petals in an unknown grave, sees Ananda creating a serene face of the skeleton Sailor, Sarath listens to the muffled cry of a woman bending over a child in a cave drawing and suddenly there is an order in the surrounding chaos with all its pains and sense of loss, things fall into place so do the responsibilities of the moment, a realigning of the private and the public spheres of existence.

The explosions and implosions in Ondaatje's texts do not end up in a chaotic scattering but there is a consistent striving for order a realignment of *the detritus of the age*, times and spaces, there is always room for negotiations, and reinventions. Ondaatje internalises architecture and archaeology into his works and the narratives are structured in a manner that they consist of the tonality of the corresponding techniques. The architectural structures in his books are not limited to buildings but Ondaatje sees architecture in books, bodies, relationships and organises the architecture of his narratives in a manner that there are reflections and counter-reflections between them – an openness that allows movement from one to other bearing a simultaneous distinctiveness and similarity of textures. Ondaatje, to an extent, does in his novels what Renee Green, the African-American artist, does through her visual arts:

> I wanted to make shapes or set up situations that are a kind of open ... . My work has a lot to do with a kind of fluidity, a movement back and forth, not making a claim to any specific or essential way of being. (qtd. by Bhabha, 3)

Renee Green's concern with shapes and situations that are kind of open also concretises Ondaatje's primary concern as an artist, he shapes his narratives in a way that they foreground a fluidity and allow a movement to and fro. The apparent commonality in the corresponding techniques of Ondaatje, a South Asian writer, and Renee Green, an African-American artist, has more to it than a mere coincidence rooted in a postmodernist approach to art. Green's emphasis on the potential of liminal spaces like a stairwell is her effort to 'make associations between certain binary divisions such as higher and lower and heaven and hell'. While Renee Green has in mind the binary racial divide between the blacks and the whites, Ondaatje tries to capture the liminal spaces between races, cultures, socio-economic hierarchies, histories, geographical spaces, disciplines, genres and the modes of being and belonging. Ondaatje's poetics is the etymological leaping out of the exile not to mourn or regret or to forget but to move through them to discover, to reinvent and recreate the self in its extensions through a constant negotiation of the contradictions and stasis.

Chelva Kanaganayakam in the context of Ghose's short story "Arrival in India" speaks of the 'camouflage,' the 'deceptive quality' that makes 'immigrant writing about a sensibility rather than a place' (Kanaganayakam, 15). The statement has a vital significance in Ondaatje's poetics. Ondaatje's treatment of different spaces speaks of a sensibility that transforms what meets the eye/I, countering static positions and leaving space for vibrant re-creations through imagination. Aamir Hussain refers to the subjective privilege in the term 'exile', "there is a tremendous inherent privilege in the term, a mobility of mind if not always of matter, to which we as writers should lay claim: a doubling instead of a split" (Kanaganayakam, 14). Ondaatje's poetics is precisely the product of this doubling, even multiplicity, the *mobility of mind* that counters the stasis of matter/space mobilising it by opening it up to reflect other spaces.

The journey of exile may both be regressive and revelatory, it can lead to a state of perennial homelessness, into a willed ghetto or may home the individual in the larger context of the world and its cultures. The exile has the privilege, the prerogative of choosing his/her path and mode of being. JanMohamed speaks of the 'specular border intellectuals' who choose to remain on the borderlines of cultures and consider 'other utopian possibilities of group formation' and the 'syncretic intellectuals' who are able to 'combine elements of the two cultures in order to articulate new syncretic forms and experiences' (JanMohamed, 97). The corresponding positions of the 'specular' and the 'syncretic' intellectuals again emphasise the crucial significance of the choice one makes, and the position one chooses to be in. Ondaatje's poetics combines the perspectives of both the specular and the syncretic intellectuals as he has chosen to create *utopian possibilities of group formations* and has also combined the elements of the two cultures of his origin and of adoption to *articulate new syncretic forms and experiences*.

The poetics of exile may acquire a more meaningful context if it is put in relation with the exile of the spiritual seeker, the exiles of Buddha. The spiritual seeker willingly moves out of the bonds of family, society and belongings to comprehend the meaning of existence, that part of the individual self that lies beyond the limits of his/her identification with a family, society, culture, time or a geographical space. Moving out of the social self is not a movement away from society or culture but it essentially enforces a deeper understanding of these constructs and endows the ability to look through them and to simultaneously capture the physical and the spiritual essence of being. Leaving his family and immediate space Buddha embraced the world and was in turn embraced by the world. Buddha cannot be reduced to an 'ism'.

Buddha is not about appropriation, but is about a surrendering, not about constriction but about expansion, not about stasis but about continuum, not about *conversion* but about perennial exploration, reinvention of the self, not about discordance but about harmony. The world has consistently defaced, has bought and placed Buddha in its museums. His statues have become invaluable for their archaicness and his timelessness hangs in abyss. Ondaatje sees this dichotomy, the overlooked obvious, in *Anil's Ghost*. The reconstruction of Buddha's statue is a reconstruction of faith, the painting of Buddha's eyes is an endowing of the lost vision to the world.

Ondaatje's latest novel *Divisadero* marks a further step in the growth of the poetics of exile. Ondaatje yet again, after *Coming Through Slaughter* and the *English Patient*, moves into a neutral or third space – the landscapes of California and France. The novel brings together some of the persistent Ondaatjean concerns – memory, history, cross-cultural movements and transformations, journeys of the self, and voyages into the self that crisscross and intermingle with the journeys and stories of the others, the multiplicity of the self and the encounters with and the escapes from one self into another. Anna's statement in the novel holds crucial clues to Ondaatje's approach:

> I come from Divisadero Street. Divisadero from the Spanish word for 'division,' the street that at one time was the dividing line between San Francisco and the fields of Presidio. Or it might derive from the word divisor, meaning 'to gaze at something from a distance.' (There is a 'height' nearby called El Divisadero.) Thus a point from which you can look far into the distance.

It is what I do with my work, I suppose. (149)

The last sentence in the above quote is significant as it reveals Ondaatje's own approach in his works. As he gets deep into the maze of the stories of different characters, times and spaces there is a simultaneous attempt to rise above them, a certain amount of distancing that would disclose unexpected connections between them and alternative possibilities.

The frame of *Divisadero* is loosely structured into three parts – 'Anna, Claire and Coop,' 'The Family in the Cart' and 'The House in Démù.' In terms of storyline, the novel has two – the stories of Anna, Claire and Coop and the story of the French writer Lucien Segura correspondingly in the landscapes of California and France. The connecting link between these two storylines is Anna whose search of the writer Lucien Segura converges into Segura's narrative. Some of reviewers have been profoundly disturbed with the structure of the novel. Benjamin Lytal in *The New York Sun*, observes:

> (H)is new novel, the strikingly odd *Divisadero*, puts him on weak footing. With an inventive structure that ought to set him apart, he sets himself adrift, trailing a flotsam of romantic scenarios. (...) Showmanship crams this book with romantic, masculine adventure.

However, it is not the first time that Ondaatje's narrative strategies have been brought into question. In Ondaatje's poetics, form remains a major concern yet it emerges only gradually, subtly subverting conventional modes of storytelling. He deliberately undermines the linear allowing the narrative and the characters to take digressions into the past and into the future.

The narrative moves sometimes in circles coming back to the point of embarking and it takes further leaps into time and space. In *Divisadero* the narrative keeps coming back to the violent incident on the farm that involved Coop, Anna and her father, something that changed their lives forever. As Anna takes a ride with her friend Branka in Dému, she wonders:

> It's like a villanelle, the inclination to go back to events in our past, the way villanelle's form refuses to move forward in linear

> development, circling instead at those familiar moments of emotion. Only the rereading counts, Nabokov said. So the strange form of the belfry, turning onto itself again and again, felt familiar to me. For we live with those retrievals from childhood that coalesce and echo throughout our lives, the way shattered pieces of glass in a kaleidoscope reappear in new forms and are songlike in their refrains and rhymes, making up a single monologue. We live permanently in the recurrence of our own stories, whatever story we tell. (142)

There are defining moments in the life of every character, moments that are decisive in setting their future courses. The tendency to return to them is not merely an act of nostalgia, the retrievals from the past and the recurrence of stories is a far more potent act; it underlies the elemental need to come to terms with the self in the present. The line in the poem Cinnamon Peeler – *as if wounded without the pleasure of a scar* – has a resonance here. Some moments in life leave permanent imprints on the soul, as it is with physical scars, with the passage of time, the heat of the emotion blurs out but the mark remains as a constant reminder of that moment, something that can be entered into and relived in a more objective manner in the present.

Each time one returns to these moments, there are newer implications, contemplation of possibilities of hidden emotions that might have existed but did not surface in the spur of the moment. The desire to judge, to fix blames is replaced by a desire to understand and to accept. Anna returns to that moment of her life:

> The discovery of us in each other's arms, under that green sky, a father attempting to murder a boy, a daughter trying to attack a father, is in retrospect something very small … . But it set fire to the rest of my life … . I have come to believe that no girl has had such an intimacy with a father … . Whatever anger existed, there must have been some grains of fearful love for me. But I did not believe that then. (146)

The moments that *set fire* to one's life, relationships and ways of being, lost in that fire find their echo in the remaining parts of an individual's life. The losses suffered in many ways govern an individual's life in the present. Anna's loss of her mother at an early age makes her an archivist:

> Those who have an orphan's sense of history love history. And my voice has become that of an orphan. Perhaps it was the unknown life of my mother, her barely drawn portrait, that made me an archivist, a historian. Because if you do not plunder the past, the absence feeds on you. (148)

Coop becomes a gambler, living in the anonymity of casinos, deliberately avoiding any permanent relationships; Claire becomes a recluse, leading an almost split life dividing it between her gruelling work for the public defendant Vea and her wild escapes into the wilderness on the weekends; Anna becomes a researcher unravelling the mysteries of archives, piecing together the almost lost lives of writers and other researchers. She feels – *I look into the distance for those I have lost, so that I see them everywhere* (149) – that is how she falls upon the life of the French writer Lucien Segura, discovering a mutual link between his life and her own:

> Nonetheless I felt there was something in the articulated voice that suggested a wound, the way one can sometimes recognize a concealed ailment in the slow movement of a king in newsreels … . There was a sweet shadow and hesitance in Segura. It was like a ruined love and it was familiar to me … . His voice with the wound in it kept haunting me. I travelled to France, to the last house he had lived in, during the final stage of his life. I pieced together the landscapes he had written about. (150)

Divisadero forms an interesting relationship with Ondaatje's earlier fiction. While there are distinctly clear echoes and intriguing continuations from his earlier novels, there is also an essential difference. It relates to the basic organisational situation; In *In the Skin of a Lion*, Patrick, Anna, Caravaggio and Small are brought together by a matter of chance, so do Almásy, Hanna, Caravaggio and Kip come together to share the space of the Italian Villa brought together by the coincidence of the War in *The English Patient*. Similarly, in *Anil's Ghost*, Anil, Sarath, Palipana and Ananda are brought together by the Civil War in Sri Lanka.

In *Divisadero* there is a reversal of sorts, while in the earlier novels characters from different spaces converge into a common space, in *Divisadero* there is dispersion from a shared space. Anna, Coop and Claire after that violent incident disperse into different directions and spaces; first as a compulsion and later as an escape. The convergence of the characters in the earlier novels and their sharing of a common space lead to new relationships and affiliations while in *Divisadero* already established relationships come under duress and as Anna, Coop, Claire and Lucien Segura take escape routes, their earlier relationships and moments that split them apart keep coming back and remain a persistent undercurrent in their psyches and govern their being in the present.

Divisadero, in many ways, is homed by orphans. Anna loses her mother at her birth, Claire is also a child of a mother who died giving birth to her and Coop too is orphaned at an early age. These three become a family as Anna's father adopts Claire and hires Coop as a farmhand. They grow up together as family, Anna and Claire as sisters and while Coop is more peripheral he stays an important link between the daughters and the father. Their ties are more affiliative than filiative as is the case in the relationships between the different characters in the earlier novels – *In the Skin of a Lion, The English Patient* and *Anil's Ghost*.

However, there is a significant difference here, as in the earlier novels these relationships are gradually established and they come at the later stages of these novels. In *Divisadero* these ties are shattered by a single incident, creating a vast vacuum at the hearts of each of the characters, maiming them for the rest of their lives. In this way their remaining lives get obsessed with escapes from the past which remains only partial as the past always finds a way to get into the present and makes it a reenactment of the moments and relationships they are trying precisely to escape from.

Anna's voyage to France to discover the life of Lucien Segura (lost in ambiguity) is her escape from her own past but it is an escape that brings her back to her past:

> This 'smallest possible space' is where Anna wishes to be now. The truth of her life comes out only in places like this. There are times when she needs to hide in a stranger's landscape, so that she can look back at the tumult of her youth, to the still-undiminished

> violence of her bloodied naked self between her father and Coop, the moment of violence that deformed her, all of them … . She can imagine her sister riding her horse in the Sierras, wearing small bells on her wrists to warn wildlife of her approach, conscious of all the possibilities of danger. Just as she herself works in archives and discovers every past but her own, again and again, because it will always be there. (80)

The desire to escape becomes a powerful motive in the novel and it brings to surface an inherent undercurrent in the poetics of exile. In Ondaatjean corpus there is a strong resistance to determinism, his characters consistently attempt to escape the traps that would incarcerate them into stasis. Billy the Kid does not stay in the same position for long and every time there is an attempt to capture him or his myth, he interposes his gun; Buddy Bolden hates to be predictable, detests 'the sure lanes of the probable'; Patrick finds escape routes into the landscapes of others; Almásy discovers the anonymity of the deserts and his own self; and Anil encounters the anonymity imposed by the power structures.

In *Divisadero* every character seems to take escape routes into the comforting zone of anonymity or into the space of others. However, unlike the earlier novels, it is more of an escape from their former selves than from determinism. It is this attempt to escape from their former selves that these characters come to believe, as Anna does, in the multiplicity of the self. Lucien Segura walks away first from his status of a well established writer into the safety of a fictitious name, writing books that nobody could associate with him and later from his family life into the anonymity of the Gers region in France. Anna remembers Nietzsche, 'We have art so that we shall not be destroyed by the truth' (279). Art provides a mask, the safety of a third person narrative to Lucien Segura and he uses it to escape from the bitterness of his marriage:

> When his marriage was dying, he found somewhere within himself the *grisette* Claudile and wrote three books about her divergent life. The fictional girl had kept him company. If this was sickness or perversion of life, it was a sickness that had helped him overcome that difficult time, and he would never demean it, or her. He would remain faithful to this person in the town of Auch whose fate he'd invented and shared with readers. (179)

Segura's escape into this unlikely fiction, his search of company in the fictional character of Claudile is interestingly his exploration of the fictional possibilities of the companionship he shared with Marie-Neige in real life. As a young man he initiated Marie-Neige into the infinite possibilities of the world of fiction, took her along with him, as he read to her, into the long adventurous journeys in the world of Dumas. And when he lost his eye, Marie became his guide into the same world. Towards the end of his career he returns to Marie in his fiction and Marie returns to him in manifold manifestations:

> She entered the story sometimes as a lover, sometimes as a sister. And in this way he spent most of his days with Marie-Neige as an ally in the court, or as a village girl who saves the hero without his being aware of it. Marie-Neige as a lost twin, Marie-Neige as a jongleuse the central character falls in love with ... . (274)

In Ondaatje's poetics the function of and concern with art finds a self-reflexive expression. It is the juxtaposition of the artistic creation with the process of creation and with life. Art seemingly provides an escape but it is more of an act of distancing, creation of a space that allows a reengagement with life. It is a simultaneous release from and fierce contention with the torturous terrains of the limitations imposed by life. Lucien Segura, a poet, transforms himself into 'La Garonne' a writer of romances apparently completely unaligned with his former self. However, there are distinct pathways that open between Lucien Segura and 'La Garonne' as there are pathways that lead from his poetry into his fiction.

Changing and reversal of roles, change of identities, assuming the skin of others and discovering the fluidity of identities frequently recur in Ondaatje's fiction. While this process for most of the characters involves an inherent struggle, there are characters who slide from one identity into another seamlessly. Caravaggio appears first in *In the Skin of a Lion* and later in *The English Patient*. He carries the name of the famous sixteenth century Italian painter and Ondaatje gives him the profession of a thief. He slips from one identity to another with remarkable ease and is instinctively aware of escape routes wherever he goes. Incidentally another character Rafael, bears the name of a great Italian painter in

Divisadero. He is not a thief himself but he is the son of a thief who never believed in any permanent names, homes or alliances except that with his wife Aria who had fathomless layers in her character. Rafael is a musician but he inherits his father's curious notions of belonging and ownership. He shies away from being owned and considers any ownership only notional in nature. He has the same approach to his music which is dominated by spontaneity:

> As a boy he had always felt that his musical lessons were a net for holding everything around him – the insects in the field, the weather shifting in the trees – so that he could give it as a collected gift, like a hand cupped with cold water held up to friend. (73)

Ondaatje's endowment of thieves' characteristics to the characters with the names of painters is a complex move. It is neither a sly reference to the craft of Caravaggio or Rafael nor is it an expression of his impression of them but on the contrary, it brings into question the commonly accepted norms of perceiving life and its possibilities. Caravaggio brought in the possibilities of blending the dramatic with the realistic into the art of painting and Rafael while drawing from nature always went a step beyond it. Ondaatje's work opens doorways from life into art and from art into life. Each challenging, questioning, complementing and opening the other in multifarious ways.

Ondaatje's poetics has come a long way from the projection of an outlaw on horseback and empty frames to an artist painting the eyes of a statue, the eyes that would make the statue, Buddha. Lucien Segura's walking away from his poetry, his success, his family with only the blue table from his past becomes emblematic of a writer's approach to his art and to life. It is neither a rejection of art nor of life but it is the manifest expression of the desire to go beyond all borders, resisting ossification in all its forms. It is an intense realisation of the infinite possibilities of life, a journey that comprehends the myth and temporality of all destinations. Here poetics of exile coalesces with the richness of poetics of life. The evolvement of Ondaatje's poetics makes the poetics of exile not just about being and belonging but about *becoming*, a fluidity that has to be felt and sustained.

Note

1. The opening excerpts are from Chelva Kanaganakayam's two papers "Writing Beyond Race: The Politics of Otherness", *The Toronto Review of Contemporary Writing Abroad*. Vol. 12. No.3. 7–16 and "A Trick with a Glass: Michael Ondaatje's South Asian Connection", *Canadian Literature* 132 (1992): 33–42.

Works Cited

Bissoondath, Neil. "The Uses of Ethnicity," *Selling Illusions: The Culture of Multiculturalism in Canada*. Toronto: Penguin 1994.

Bhabha, Homi. *The Locations of Culture*. London: Routledge, 1994.

JanMohamed, Abdul R. "Worldliness-without-World, Homelessness-as-Home: Towards a Definition of the Specular Border Intellectual," *Edward Said: A Critical Reader*. Oxford: Blackwell. 1992

Kanaganakayam, Chelva. "A Trick With Glass: Michael Ondaatje's South Asian Connection," *Canadian Literature*. Vol. 132 (1992): 33–34.

Lytal, Benjamin. Review. *The New York Sun*. 23.5.2007.

Mishra, Vijay. "Diasporas and the Art of Impossible Mourning", *In Diaspora: Theories, Histories, Texts*. Ed. Makarand Paranjape, New Delhi: Indialog, 2001.

Ondaatje, Michael. *Divisadero*, London: Bloomsbury, 2008.

Van Herk, Aritha. "Writing the Immigrant Self: Disguise and Damnation." *In Visible Ink*. Edmonton: Newest Press, 1991.

Bibliography

Primary Sources

The Dainty Monsters. Toronto: Coach House, 1967.

The Man With Seven Toes. Toronto: Coach House, 1969

The Collected Works of Billy the Kid: Left Handed Poems. Toronto: House of Anansi, 1970.

Leonard Cohen. Canadian Writers series, No. 5 Toronto: McClelland and Stewart, 1970.

The Broken Ark: A Book of Beasts (Ed.). Ottawa: Oberon, 1971

Rat Jelly. Toronto: Coach House, 1973.

Coming Through Slaughter. Toronto: House of Anansi, 1976.

Personal Fictions: Stories by Muillo, Wiebe, Thomas and Blais (Ed.). Toronto: Oxford Univ. Press, 1977

The Long Poem Anthology (Ed.). Toronto: Coach House, 1979.

There's a Trick With a Knife I'm Learning to Do: *Poems* 1963–1978. Toronto: McClelland and Stewart, 1979.

Running in the Family. Toronto: McClelland and Stewart, 1982.

Secular Love. Toronto: Coach House, 1984.

In the Skin of a Lion. Toronto: McClelland and Stewart, 1987.

Russell Banks and David Young, Eds. *Brushes with Greatness: An Anthology of Chance Encounters with Celebrities*. Toronto: Coach House. 1989.

The Cinnamon Peeler: Selected Poems, 1989. Toronto: McClelland, 1992.

From Ink Lake: *Canadian Stories* (Ed.). Toronto: Lester & Orphen Dennys, 1990.

The English Patient, Toronto: McClelland, 1992.

Handwriting, Toronto: McClelland and Stewart, 1998.

Anil's Ghost, New Delhi: Picador India, 2000.

Divisadero, London: Bloomsbury, 2008.

Films

Sons of Captain Poetry, Cameraman Robert Fresco. Mongrel Films/ Canadian Film-Makers Distribution Centre, 1970. (16 mm.; colour; 35 min.)

Carry on Crime and Punishment, Mongrel Films; 1972. (16 mm.; 5 min.)

——. prod. and sir. *The Clinton Special.* Cameramen Bob Carney and Robert Fresco. Mongrel.

Films/Canadian Film-makers Distribution Centre, 1972. (16 mm.; 71 min.; colour).

Secondary Sources

Adachi, Ken. "Legendary Jazzman's Slides to Madness an Intriguing Collage." *The Toronto Star*. 20 Nov. 1976, p. F 9.

——. "A Memoir Illuminated by Imagination." *The Toronto Star*. 9 Oct. 1982, p. F 10.

Ahmed, Aijaz. *In Theory*: *Classes, Nations, Literatures*. London: Verso, 1992.

Albert, Richard. Int. *From Blues to Bop*: *A Collection of Jazz Fiction*. Ed. Albert, Baton Rouge. Louisiana State UP, 1990. pp. 1–7.

Archer, Anne. Rev. of *There's a Trick with a Knife I'm Learning to Do: Poems* 1963–1978. *Quarry,* 29, No. I, Winter, 1980: 77–79.

Ashcroft, Bill, Gareth Griffiths and Helen Tiffin. *The Empire Writers Back*: *Theory and Practice in Post-Colonial Literatures*. New Accents. London : Routledge, 1989.

——. *Key Concepts in Post-Colonial Studies*. London: Routledge, 1998.

Atwood, Margaret. *Survival*: *A Thematic Guide to Canadians Literature*. Toronto: House of Anansi, 1972, pp. 76, 84.

——. Introduction. In *The New Oxford Book of Canadian Verse. In English* Ed. Margaret Atwood. Toronto: OUP, 1982, pp. xxiii, xxxviii.

Balliett, Whitney. Rev. of *Running in the Family. The New Yorker,* 27 Dec. 1982, pp. 76–77.

Barbour, Douglas. "The Last Time I wrote "Paris": Ondaatje's First Attempt at a Poetic Sequence in "Troy Town." *ECW* 53 (Summer, 1994), p. 107.

——. "Controlling the Jungle." *Canadian Literature,* 36 (Spring, 1968), pp. 83–88.

Barrie, B.D. Rev. of *Rat Jelly. The Fiddlehead,* No.98 (Summer, 1973), pp. 119–20.

Beddoes, Julie. "Books Will Long Shelf Life." Review of *Running in the Family,* by Michael Ondaatje; and *Incognito* by David Young. *Flare,* 5, No. 4 (May, 1983), pp. 59–60.

Bennett, Donna, and Russell Brown. "Michael Ondaatje, B. 1943." In *An Anthology of Canadian Literature in English.* Ed. Donna Bennett and Russell Brown. Vol. II. Toronto : OUP, 1983, pp. 569–70.

Beran, Carol L. "Ex-Centricity: Michael Ondaatje's *In the Skin of a Lion* and Hugh Maclennan's *Barometer Rising.*" *SCL/ELC*, Vol. 16.2. (1992), pp. 71–83.

Berger, Carl. *The Writing of Canadian History: Aspects of English-Canadian Historical Writing Since 1900.* 2nd ed. Toronto: University of Toronto Press. 1986.

Bhabha, Homi K. *Locations of Culture*. London: Routledge, 1994.

Bishop, E.L. Review of *Coming Through Slaughter, Quarry,* 26, No. I (Winter, 1977), p. 149.

Bissoondath, Neil. "The Uses of Ethnicity", *Selling Illusions: The Culture of Multiculturalism in Canada*. Toronto: Penguin 1994.

Blott, Anne. "Stories to Finish: *The Collected Works of Billy the Kid*". *Studies in Canadian Literature,* 2 (Summer, 1977), pp. 188–202.

——. "Michael Ondaatje 1943". In *Canadian Poetry.* Ed. Jack David and Robert Lecker. Introduction George Woodcock. New Press Canadian Classics. Toronto/ Downsview, Ont.: General/ECW, 1982. Vol. II, pp. 317–18.

Bok, Christian. "The Politicization of Violence in the Works of Michael Ondaatje." *Canadian Literature* 132 (1992), pp. 109–24.

Bourjaily, Vance. "In and Out of Stroryville: Jazz and Fiction." *New York Times Book Review.* 13 Dec. 1987 : I, pp. 44–45.

Bowering, George. "The Painted Window: Notes on Post-Realist Fiction." *The University of Windsor Review,* 13, No. 2 (Spring Summer, 1978), p. 28.

Braydon. Diana. "Making the Present Continuous." *Canadian Literature.* No. 86 (Autumn, 1980), pp. 99–100.

______. and Helen, Tiffin. *Decolonising Fictions.* Sydney: Dangaroo, 1993.

Brown, Dee. *The American West.* New York: Charles Scribner's Sons, 1994.

Butscher, E. Rev. of *There's a Trick with a Knife I'm Learning to Do: Poems* 1963–1978. *Booklist.* I. May 1979, p.341.

Butterfield, Martha. "The One Lighted Room: *In the Skin of a Lion*". *Canadian Literature,* No. 119 (Winter, 1988). pp. 162–167.

Chamberlin, J.E. "Let There be Commerce Between Us: The Poetry of Michael Ondaatje". *Descant.* No. 42. 14, No. 4 (Fall, 1983), pp. 89–98.

Clarke, George. "Michael Ondaatje and the Production of Myth." *Studies in Canadian Literature.* 16, No. I (Spring, 1991), pp. 1–21.

Cogswell, Fred. Rev. of *The Collected Works of Billy the Kid: Left Handed Poems. The Fiddlehead.* No. 88 (Winter, 1971), pp. 105–06.

Coleman, Daniel. "Masculinity's Severed Self: Gender and Orientalism in *Out of Egypt* and *Running in the Family*". *SCL/ELC* Vol. 17.2 (1993): , pp. 63–79.

Collier, John. *Indians of the Americas*: New York Mentor Books, 1975.

Collins, R.G. and John Wortley, Eds. *The Literature of Exile.* Canada: University of Manitoba Press, 1975.

Cook, Rufus. "Imploding Time and Geography: Narrative Compressions in Michael Ondaatje's *The English Patient*". *Journal of Commonwealth Literature*. No. 2. (1996), pp. 109–125.

Cooley, Dennis. "*I Am Here on the Edge:* Modern Hero/Postmodern Poetics in *The Collected Works of Billy the Kid.*" Solecki, *Spider Blues* (1985), pp. 211–39.

Cooper, Fenimore. *The Last of the Mohicans*. Bridlington: Priory Classics, 1982.

Davenport, Guy. "The Symbol of the Archaic." *The Geography of the Imagination: Forty Essays by Guy Davenport.* San Francisco: North Point, 1981. pp. 16–28.

Davey, Frank. "Michael Ondaatje (1943)". In his *From There to Here: A Guide to English Canadian Literature since 1960.* Vol. II of *Our Nature – Our Voices.* Erin, ant. : Porcepic, 1974, pp. 222–27.

David, Jack. "Michael Ondaatje's *The Collected Works of Billy the Kid*". *Canadian Notes & Quarries,* No. 13 (June, 1974), pp. 11–12.

Davis, Marilyn. Rev. of *The Collected Works of Billy the Kid: Left Handed Poems. The Canadian Forum* (July–August, 1971), pp. 34–35.

Denisoff, Dennis. "Homosocial Desire and the Artificial Man in Michael Ondaatje's *The Collected Works of Billy the Kid. Michael Ondaatje Issue, ECW,* No. 53 (Summer, 1994), pp. 51–70.

Derksen, Celeste. "Masculanity and the Mise En Scene: *The Collected Works of Billy the Kid*". *SCL/ELC.* Vol. 20. No. 2 (1995), pp. 22–33.

Draper, Gary. "Stranger Than Fiction". *Books in Canada.* Dec. 1982. pp. 19–20.

Eder, Richard. "Triumph of Blurred Memory." *The Vancouver Sun.* 15 Oct. 1982, Sec. Insight, p. L25.

Enright, Robert. "Poetry Notes". *CV/II,* 2, No. 3 (Aug., 1976), p. 3.

Farley, T.E. *Exiles and Pioneers: Two Visions of Canada's Future* 1825–1975. Ottawa: Borealis, 1976, pp. 193–94.

Fernstron, Ken. Rev. of *The Long Poem Anthology. Quill & Quire.* March 1980, p. 62.

Ferris, Ina. "Michael Ondaatje and the Turn to Narrative". *Canadian Writers and Their Works.* Ed. Robert Lecker, Jack David and Ellen Quigley. ECW Press, 1992.

Fisher, Michael M.J. "Ethnicity and the Post-Modern Arts of Memory". *Writing Culture: The Poetics and Politics of Ethnography.* Ed. James Clifford and George E. Marcus. Berkeley: University of California Press, 1986. pp. 194–233.

Fledderus, Bill "The English Patient Reposed in his Bed Like a (Fisher?) King: Elements of Grail Romance in Ondaatje's *The English Patient.*" *SCL/ELC.* Vol. 22.1 (1997), p. 48.

Foucault, Michel. "Texts/Contexts: Of Other Spaces". *Diacritics,* Spring 1986.

Frantz, Joe B. *The American Cowboy: The Myth and Reality.* Westport, CT: Greenwood Press, 1981.

French, William. "A Portrait or a Gesture, Michael Ondaatje's Discovery of His Family Roots Is a Remarkable Work." *The Globe and Mail* (Toronto), 9 Oct. 1982, p. 15.

Gallager, Noel. "Ondaatje Still Part of London Literary Community." *The London Free Press,* 6 April 1979, p. D6.

Geddes, Gary, and Phyllis Bruce. "Michael Ondaatje". In *15 Canadian Poets.* Ed. and preface Gary Geddes and Phyllis Bruce. Toronto: Oxford Univ. Press, 1970. pp. 287–89.

Gibaldi, Joseph. *MLA Handbook for Writers of Research Papers.* New Delhi: EWP, 1996.

Giddins, Gary. *Rhythm-a-ning.. Jazz Tradition and Innovation in the 80's.* New York: Oxford University Press. 1986.

Giedion, Sigfried. *Space, Time and Architecture: The Growth of a New Tradition.* Trans. W.J. Callaghan and E. Matthews. Cambridge: Harvard University Press. 1941.

Gioia, Ted. *The History of Jazz.* New York: OUP, 1997.

Girard, Rene. *Violence and the Sacred.* London: The John Hopkins University Press, 1972.

Gnarowski, Michael. "Ondaatje Michael 1943". In his *A Concise Bibliography of English Canadian Literature.* Toronto: McClelland and Stewart, 1973. pp. 89–90. Rev. ed. 1978. p. 105

Greenstein, Michael. "Ondaatje's Metamorphoses: *In the Skin of a Lion*". *Canadian Literature.* No. 126 (Autumn, 1990) pp. 116–30.

Hancock, Geeff. Rev. of *Coming Through Slaughter: The Malahat Review,* No. 44 (Oct., 1977), pp. 140–42.

Harding- Russell. Gillian. "A Note on Ondaatje's *Peter:* A Creative Myth." *Canadian Literature.* No. 112 (Spring, 1987), p. 205.

Heble, Ajay. "Michael Ondaatje and the Problem of History". *Clio.* No. 19 (Winter, 1990), pp. 97–100.

——. "Rumours of Topography": The Cultural Politics of Michael Ondaatje's *Running in the Family. Michael Ondaatje Issue.* Ed. Karen E. Smythe. Special Issue of *Essays on Canadian Writing.* 53 (1994), pp. 186–203.

——. "Putting Together Another Family: *In the Skin of a Lion,* Affiliation, and the Writing of Canadian (Hi)stories." *Essays on Canadian Writing* 56 (Fall, 1995), pp. 236–54.

Heigton, Stephen. "Approaching *that Perfect Edge:* Kinetic Techniques in the Poetry and Fiction of Michael Ondaatje." *Studies in Canadian Literature.* 13, No.2 (Summer, 1988), pp. 223–43.

Huggan, Graham. "Exoticism and Ethnicity in Michael Ondaatje's *Running in the Family.*" *Essays on Canadian Writing.* No. 57 (Winter, 1995), pp. 116–27.

Hutcheon, Linda. "*Snow Storm of Paper*: The Act of Reading in Self-Reflexive Canadian Verse." *Dalhousie Review*. 59 (Spring, 1979), 116–17.

——. *A Poetics of Postmodernism: History, Theory, Fiction* New York: Routledge, 1988.

——. *The Canadian Postmodern*: *A Study of Contemporary English -Canadian Fiction*. Toronto: Oxford University Press. 1988.

——. "*Running in the Family*: The Postmodernist Challenge." *Spider Blues*. Ed. Sam Solecki. Montreal: Vehicule Press, 1985, pp. 301–14.

——. "Ex-Centric." *Canadian Literature* 1147 (1988), pp. 132–35.

Jacobs, Naomi. "Michael Ondaatje and the New Fiction Biographies." *Studies in Canadian Literature*. II No. I (Spring, 1986), pp. 2–18.

Jain, Jasbir. Ed. *Writers of the Indian Diaspora*. Jaipur and New Delhi: Rawat Publications, 1998.

JanMohamed, Abdul R. "Worldliness-without-World, Homeless-ness-as-Home: Towards a Definition of the Specular Border Intellectual", *Edward Said: A Critical Reader*. Oxford: Blackwell. 1992.

Jarrett, Michael. "Writing Mystory: *Coming Through Slaughter*". *Michael Ondaatje Issue ECW*, No. 53 (Summer, 1994), p. 42.

Jewinski, Ed. *Express Yourself Beautifully*. ECW Press, 1998.

Jones, Manina. "*Collected Works of Billy the Kid*: Scripting the *Docudrama*". *Canadian Literature*. Nos. 122–23 (Autumn-Winter, 1989), pp. 26–38.

——. "So Many Varieties of Murder": Detection and Biography in *Coming Through Slaughter*." *ECW* . No. 53. (Summer, 1994), , pp. 11–26.

Kahn, Sy. Rev. of *The Dainty Monsters. Far Point*. I (Fall-Winter, 1968), pp. 70–76.

Kamboureli, Smaro. "Outlawed Narrative: Michael Ondaatje's *The Collected Works of Billy the Kid*." *Sagetrieble* 0, 7, No. I (Spring, 1988), pp. 115–29.

Kanaganakayam, Chelva. "A Trick With Glass: Michael Ondaatje's South Asian Connection." *Canadian Literature*. Vol. 132 (1992), pp. 33–34.

Kertzer, Jon. Rev. of *Coming Through Slaughter: The Fiddlehead*. No. 113 (Spring, 1977), pp. 126–29.

Kipling, Rudyard. *Kim*. Wordsworth Classics, 1993.

Klinck, Carl F. and Reginald E. Watters. "Michael Ondaatje (1943)" In *Canadian Anthology* Ed. Carl F. Klinck and Reginald E. Watters. 3rd ed. Toronto: Gage, 1974, p. 578.

Kroetsch, Robert. "The Exploding Porcupine: Violence of Form in English-Canadian Fiction". In *Violence in the Canadian Novel Since 1960/dans Ie roman candien depuis 1960* Ed. Virginia Harger-Grinling and Terry Goldie. St. John's: Memorial University (1981). pp. 194–99.

Lecker, Robert A Rev. of *Coming Through Slaughter. Quill & Quire.* (Nov., 1976), p. 32.

Lee, Dennis. *Savage Fields: An Essay* in *Literature and Cosmology.* Toronto: House of Anansi, 1977, pp. 4. 15–60, 115–22.

Leith, Linda. "Serendipity." Rev. of *In the Skin of a Lion. The Canadian Forum* (Aug.–Sept., 1987), pp. 35–37.

Logan, William. Rev. of *There's a Trick With a Knife I'm Learning to Do: Poems* 1963–78. *Library Journal.* I April 1979, p. 833.

Lower, AR. M. "The Case against Immigration." *Queens Quarterly.* i37 (1930), pp. 557–74.

Loomba, Ania. *Colonialism/Postcolonialism.* London: Routledge, 1998.

MacIntyre, Ernest. "Outside of Time: *Running in the Family.*" *Spider Blues: Essays on Michael Ondaatje* Ed. Sam Solecki. Montreal: Vehicule. 1985. pp. 315–19.

MacLulich, T.D. "Ondaatje's Mechanical Boy: Portrait of the Artist as Photographer." *Mosaic: A Journal for the Comparative Study of Literature and Ideas* 14, No.2 (Spring, 1981), pp. 107–19.

Mandel, Eli. "Modern Canadian Poetry." *Twentieth Century Literature.* 16 (July, 1970), p. 181.

Marshall, Tom. *Harsh and Lovely Land: The Major Canadian Poets and the Making of a Canadian Tradition,* Vancouver: University of British Columbia Press, 1979, pp. xiv, 112, 123–26, 144–47, 149, 15354,163–64,167–70,172.

Maxwell, Barry. "Surrealistic Aspects of Michael Ondaatje's *Coming Through Slaughter.*" *Mosaic,* 18, No.3 (Summer, 1985): 101–14.

Miller, Danielle "Postmodernism: Bourgeois Smoke Screen of Ethical Philosophy. A Comparison Michael Ondaatje's *Coming Through Slaughter* and Hubert Aquin's *Neige Noire*". *British Journal of Commonwealth Studies.* Vol.8, No. 2 (1993), p. 217.

Mishra, Vijay. "Diasporas and the Art of Impossible Mourning", *In Diaspora: Theories, Histories, Texts.* Ed. Makarand Paranjape. New Delhi: Indialog, 2001.

Moss, John. *A Reader's Guide to the Canadian Novel.* Toronto: McClelland and Stewart, 1981, pp. 22324, 355, 360, 362, 363, 365.

Mukherjee, Arun. "The Poetry of Michael Ondaatje and Cyril Dabydeen: Two Responses to Otherness". *Journal of Canadian Literature* 20, No. I (Spring, 1985), pp. 49–67.

——. *Towards an Aesthetic of Opposition Essays on Literature Criticism and Cultural Imperialism.* Stratford, Ontario: Williams-Wallace 1988.

Mundwiler, Leslie. *Michael Ondaatje: Word, Image, Imagination.* Vancouver: Talonbooks, 1984.

Nodelman, Perry. "The Collected Photographs of Billy the Kid". *Canadian Literature,* No. 87 (Winter, 1980), pp. 68–79.

Norris, Ken. "The Architecture of *Secular Love:* Michael Ondaatje's Journey into the Confessional." *Michael Ondaatje Issue. ECW,* No. 53 (Summer, 1994), pp. 43–50.

Overbye, Karen. "Re-Membering the Body: Constructing the Self as Hero in *In the Skin of a Lion*", *SCL/ELC.* Vol. 17.2 (1993), p. 12.

Packer, George. "Refractions." Rev. of *In the Skin of Lion* by Michael Ondaatje. *Nation* 17 Oct. 1987, pp. 421–22.

Polley, Jane. Ed. *The Reader's Digest Book of American Folklore and Legend.* 1978.

Porter, John. "A Canadian Nobel Prize Winner?" *Academy of Canadian Writers Newsletter,* 2, No. 2 (Feb., 1981), p. 2.

Prator, Ed. "A Net Full of Ondaatje." *Canadian Literature,* No. 87 (Winter, 1980), pp. 103–05.

Ramerini, Marco. "History of the Dutch in Ceylon (Sri Lanka): The Burgher of Ceylon", www.lankalibrary.com

Roosevelt, Karyl. Rev. of *The Collected Works of Billy the Kid: Left Handed Poems. The New York Times Book Review.* (17 Nov., 1974), p. 49.

Russell, J. "Travel Memoir as Nonfiction Novel: Michael Ondaatje's *Running in the Family.*" *Ariel,* No. 22 (April, 1991), pp. 23–40.

Said, Edward W. *Culture and Imperialism* New York: Knopf, 1993.

Schmitz, Neil. Rev. of *In the Skin of a Lion. Queen's Quarterly,* 95, No.2 (Summer, 1988), pp. 452–54.

Scobie, Stephen. "Two Authors in Search of a Character". *Canadian Literature.* No. 54 (Autumn, 1972), pp. 37–55.

——. "His Legend a Jungle Sleep: Michael Ondaatje and Henri Rousseau." *Canadian Literature.* No. 76 (Spring, 1978), pp. 6–21.

——. "*Coming Through Slaughter:* Fictional Magnets and Spider's Webbs". *Essays on Canadian Writing:* No. 12 (Fall, 1978), pp. 5–23.

——. Rev. of *Rat Jelly. World Literature Written in English,* 13 (Nov., 1974), pp. 279–82.

——. Rev. of *There's a Trick with a Knife I'm Learning to Do: Poems 1963–78. The Fiddlehead:* No. 129 (Spring, 1981), pp. 100–02.

——. "The Lies Stay In: A Review of *There's a Trick with a Knife I'm Learning to Do*". Ed. Solecki, *Spider Blues* (1985), pp. 117–20.

——. "The Reading Lesson: Michael Ondaatje and the Patients of Desire." *ECW,* No. 53 (Summer, 1994), pp. 92–106.

——. "The Heart Is an Organ of Fire". *The World and I.* (Feb., 1993), pp. 301–09.

Slemon, Stephen. "Magic Realism as Post-Colonial Discourse". *Canadian Literature.* 116 (1988), pp. 9–24.

Smith, Patricia Keeney. "Michael Ondaatje: A Poet Sets the Stage". *Performing Arts in Canada.* 18, No. 4 (Winter, 1981), p. 45.

Soderlind, Sylvia. "The Contest of Marginalities". *Essays on Canadian Writing.* No. 56 (1995), pp. 96–109.

Soja, Edward W. *Postmodern Geographies: The Reassertion of Space in Critical Theory.* Jaipur and New Delhi: Rawat Publications. 1997.

Solecki, Sam. "Nets and Chaos: The Poetry of Michael Ondaatje". *Studies in Canadian Literature.* 2 (Winter, 1977), pp. 36–48.

——. "Making and Destroying: Michael Ondaatje's *The Man With Seven Toes.*" *Canadian Poetry: Studies, Documents, Reviews,* No. 6 (Spring-Summer, 1980), pp. 14–24.

——. "Michael Ondaatje." *Descant.* No. 42. 14, No.4 (Fall, 1983), pp. 77–78.

——. "Sharpening His Act." *Books In Canada.* (June–July, 1979), 2.

——. "Michael Ondaatje: A Paper Promiscuous and out of Form with Several Inlargements and Untutored Narrative." *Descant.* 14.4 (1983), pp. 77–88.

——. Ed. *Spider Blues: Essays on Michael Ondaatje.* Montreal: Vehicule, 1985.

Spearey, Susan. "Mapping and Masking: The Migrant Experience in Michael Ondaatje's *In the Skin of the Lion.*" *Journal of Commonwealth Literature.* No. 1. (1995), pp. 45–59.

Story, Narah. "Poetry in English." In her *The Oxford Companion to Canadian History and Literature.* Toronto: Oxford University Press, 1967, p. 651.

Stevens, Peter. Rev. of *Collected Works of Billy the Kid. Queens's Quarterly*. Vol. 78 (Summer, 1971), pp. 326–27.

Struthers, Betry. Rev. of *There's a Trick with a Knife I'm Learning to Do: Poems* 1963–78. *Canadian Book Review Annual:* 1979. Ed. Dean Tudor, Nancy Tudor and Kathy Vanderlinden. Toronto: PMA, 1980, p. 143.

Sugunasiri, Suwanda H.J. "SriLankan Canadian Poets: The Bourgeoisie that Fled the Revolution". *Canadian Literature*. Vol. 132 (1992), pp. 60–79.

Surette, Leon. Rev. of *Coming Through Slaughter. Canadian Fiction Magazine* Nos. 24–25 (Spring, 1977), pp. 165–67.

Sward, Robert. Rev. of *Running in the Family Cross-Canada Writers Quarterly,* 5, No. I (1983), pp. 23–24.

Testa, Bart. "He Did Not Work Here for Long: Michael Ondaatje in the Cinema". *ECW*. No.53. (Summer, 1994), p. 154.

Tiffin, Helen. "Post-Colonialism, Post-Modernism and the Rehabilitation of Post-Colonial History". *Journal of Commonwealth Literature,* 23 (1988), pp. 169–81.

Thompson, Kent. Rev. of *The Dainty Monsters. The Fiddlehead,* No. 75, Spring, 1968, pp. 67–68.

Toye, William. Ed. *The Oxford Companion to Canadian Literature*. Toronto: OUP, 1983.

Turner, Barbara. "In the Skin of Michael Ondaatje : Giving Voice to a Social Conscience." *Quill and Quire,* May 1987, pp. 21–22.

Van Herk, Aritha. Rev. of *In the Skin of a Lion* by Michael Ondaatje. *Malahat* Review 80 (1987), pp. 134–37.

——. "Writing the Immigrant Self: Disguise and Damnation." *In Visible Ink*. Newest Press: Edmonton, 1991.

Van Wart, Alice. "The Evolution of Form in Michael Ondaatje's *The Collected Works of Billy the Kid* and *Coming Through Slaughter*". *Canadian Poetry: Studies, Documents, Reviews* No. 17 (Fall-Winter, 1985), pp. 1–28.

Vevaina, Coomi S. "Erasing Edges: Michael Ondaatje's *Coming Through Slaughter* and *Running in the Family* as Postmodernist Fiction." *Postmodernism and Feminism: Canadian Contexts*. Ed. Shrin Kudchedkar. New Delhi: Pencraft International, 1995, p. 42.

Waterston, Elizabeth. *Survey: A Short History of Canadian Literature*. Methuen Canadian Literature Series. Toronto: Methuen, 1973, pp. 88, 133.

Watson, Sheila. "Michael Ondaatje: The Mechanization Death". *White Pelican*. 2, No. 4 (Fall, 1972), pp. 56–64.

Wilson, Ann. "*Coming Through Slaughter:* Storyville Twice Told." *Descant*. No. 42 (Fall, 1983), pp. 99–111.

Woodcock, George. "Poetry." In *Literary History of Canada*: *Canadian Literature in English*. Gen. Ed. and introd. Carl F. Klinck 2nd ed. Toronto: University of Toronto Press, 1979. Va. III, p. 286, 289, 296, 297,314.

Yardley, Jonathan. "*Lost White Tribes* by Ricardo Orizio", www.wehaitians.com, Sunday, July 22, 2001; Page BW02.

York, Lorraine M. "Whirling Blindfolded in the House of Women: Gender Politics in the Poetry and Fiction of Michael Ondaatje". *ECW*. No. 53 (Summer, 1994), pp. 71–79.

Zepetnek, Stevens T. "*The English Patient*: "Truth is Stranger Than Fiction", *ECW*. No. 53 (Summer, 1994), p. 141.

Interviews

Barbour, Douglas and Stephen Scobie. "A Conversation with Michael Ondaatje." *White Pelican*. I. No. 2 (Spring, 1971), pp. 6–15.

Hutcheon, Linda. "Michael Ondaatje" (Interview) *Other Solitudes*: *Canadian Multicultural Fictions*. Ed. Hutcheon and Marion Richmond Toronto: Oxford University Press, 1990, pp. 179–202.

"Michael Ondaatje: An Interview by Catherine Bush". *Conjuctions* 15 (1990), pp. 87–98.

Index